TRUST
AGENTS

TRUST AGENTS

USING THE WEB TO **BUILD INFLUENCE, IMPROVE REPUTATION,** AND **EARN TRUST**

CHRIS BROGAN AND JULIEN SMITH

WILEY

John Wiley & Sons, Inc.

HF
5415.1265
.B75
2009

To Kat and the kids, who suffer the most for my passions.
—CB

To my parents, who showed me the way.
—JS

Contents

Acknowledgments

Thanks to Shannon "Queen of All Things Book" Vargo, Matt "Dive Bar Finder" Holt, Ellen "Why don't you have a book deal?" Gerstein, and Chris "This won't hurt a bit" Webb from John Wiley and Sons. Thanks also to Jeff "Believe in Yourself" Pulver and countless others who believed.

Introduction:
Hey, I Know You.
Have We Met?

We have some ideas about you, and we were curious to see whether they're correct. If you're reading this book, you're most likely a business professional, perhaps a small business owner, or maybe someone in marketing, public relations, or some other communications world. Or perhaps you're a technologist, such as a Web designer or a software engineer. If you are, you're the kind who acts as that amazing bridge between the bosses and the gearheads. Are we right?

You might be the "social media evangelist," official or otherwise, at your organization (big or small). You read some blogs. You might even subscribe to a few podcasts, and you know the difference between a wiki and a Twitter. Your official title doesn't necessarily match this passion, but you're looking for a way to take advantage of some kind of opportunity that lets you do this kind of stuff for business.

Perhaps you've been noticing that the older approach to marketing, PR, advertising, business communication, and other activities on the Web aren't pulling as well as they used to, and you're wondering what comes next. You've read all about how you should be "joining the conversation" and how "Web 2.0 is about the wisdom of crowds." While you're not entirely sure what to do next, you're very sure that people no longer blindly respond to typical advertisements or other traditional marketing.

In short, you've come to this book looking to improve yourself and, specifically, to improve how you do business over the Web.

The Web has changed to be more humanized, and the people who will succeed in understanding this and using the Web to build business are called *trust agents*.

We're here to help you become one of them.

What the Book Is About

Trust Agents is the answer to the question, "What do I do now?" It is full of actionable information, supported by research and strategies, studies, and an explanation of the thought process behind what we do on the Web. We love all the great "idea" books out there, and we do have *lots* of ideas packed in here as starting points. In addition to these, we give you *actionable* tasks you can execute.

The idea for this book came out of our individual successes in achieving goals using the Web to work with people and out of our fascination with non-currency-based economies. We've taken what we've learned from our years as "digital natives" (people who have grown up inhabiting the various online haunts of the moment), combined it with our understanding of games, people, and business as a whole, and followed it all up with information and ideas to help you better understand the mindset required to match these actions to your business needs. Said another way, we can tell you what we do and how we do it, but you might have to tinker a bit with the recipe for it to work directly for your business.

In early 2008, we wrote a manifesto titled *Trust Economies*, using an online publisher called ChangeThis, which focuses on groundbreaking, new ideas. It's in *Trust Economies* that we started to sketch out some of the concepts that have evolved since the inception of this book. Humans, it turns out, are motivated by rewards, just like many animals; and the rewards don't always have to be as basic as money, food, sex, or sleep. Rewards—and the value we ascribe to them—sometimes relate to matters other than just money. For example, Chris's blog is among the top that are linked to in the world, but that doesn't help his bottom line (at least, not directly).

It's that last part that interests us most. The way the Web works isn't always direct, either. But those who understand social proof, social capital, and how people use alternative reward systems and alternative currencies are part of the story. We've discovered that people who understand how to build relationships on the Web also know how to make business happen using this understanding.

What You Can Expect

The first chapter of *Trust Agents* will give you a sense of trust, social capital, and media. In the first chapter, we intend for you to get comfortable with some of the levers we move to change outcomes.

The next six chapters explain these six basic principles of being a trust agent. You're likely doing a few of these things already. For example, if you've realized that your LinkedIn profile provides you more potential business opportunities once you have more testimonials and recommendations on your profile, you have practiced "making your own game." You may be someone within your social circle whom others respect and trust to make recommendations on products. If so, you've practiced becoming "one of us."

In fact, it is likely that part of the reason you picked up this book is *because* you're doing lots of this already. You have an affinity for this type of activity, and now you want to see what else you can add to your arsenal. Either that or you're completely new to these concepts and someone has handed this book to you (or you picked it up yourself) with the hope that you can build up your business using the ideas, techniques, and actions inside. We can help you with that, too.

Why This Book Is about Business and Not Technology

We'll discuss all kinds of software and technology—cutting-edge as well as tried-and-true—that we use to do business on the Web. It's not exactly the technology du jour that one should focus on, because technologies come and go. For example, though e-mail has been around for decades, people continue to use e-mail marketing as part of how they do business. Services like Facebook and Twitter and blogs and podcasts are some of the more recent resources. They enable human-scale communication, and they are part of what feeds the larger Web, tools that help you conduct business in a strategic fashion.

So, try not to focus on the tools. Instead, put your energy into learning how these tools encourage certain interactions, how they might be leveraged to build different types of experiences with potential customers, with competitors, with the very fabric of how the Web's information is wired. Focus on connecting with the people, and the tools will all make sense.

Who We Are

To write a book about trust, it might be good to introduce ourselves.

Chris Brogan's blog (chrisbrogan.com) is ranked by Technorati as one of the top 100 blogs in the world. *Advertising Age's* Power 150 ranks him in the top 15. He has blogged since 1998 (back when it was called *journaling*). Chris is also the co-founder of the international new media conference series PodCamp (founded with Christopher S. Penn). Before he began all this, his background was in telecommunications and enterprise technology, where he did everything from customer service to software deployment engineering to project management and beyond.

Julien Smith has been connecting with computers since the age of 12. He helped run early BBSes (local message boards into which you had to call by using a phone line) and was among the first people to start podcasting and make a living from it. He has run a ton of online communities, from forums to early flash mobs. He is a specialist in developing human connections and in understanding systems.

We met in 2005 at the first ever PodCamp and immediately realized that we both had a certain affinity for figuring things out. Chris tends to work more toward understanding how humans will help him reach a goal, whereas Julien tends to figure out how the Web works mechanically toward achieving a similar goal. That doesn't mean Julien isn't personable, and it doesn't mean Chris isn't technical. Rather, when faced with a complex challenge, we tend to focus our efforts in our respective areas of strength. Both approaches are required skill sets in a trust agent.

As with everything we do, we encourage you to ask others about us. Ask Google. See what you can drag up on your own. If you're the trust agent we believe you are, you already have a sense that the Web can help tell part of the story, and you know that it will lead you to see what others say about us. Why trust us when you can ask the entire Web?

Related to that very point, let's discuss trust and how humans understand such things. And let's start at a time before Google.

1

Trust, Social Capital, and Media

The Connected Guy

Joe Pistone had thought he was going to go undercover for six months. Instead, he vanished for six years.

You see, he was already practically a wiseguy. He had grown up among the Mafia in Paterson, New Jersey, and had worked the same kind of jobs. Like many involved in the Mob, Pistone was of Sicilian descent and spoke Italian, and they accepted him. When he started showing up at Carmello's—a restaurant at 1638 York Avenue on the corner of 86th Street and one block from the East River—he fit in perfectly. He knew it was a spot in Manhattan where wiseguys hung out, and he knew he'd get acquainted eventually. He just didn't know how deep he would get.

Turns out that, to go undercover, Pistone knew how to make all the right moves. He knew that in order to be a good undercover agent, he needed to be a good street agent: someone who understood not just how things worked in an office, but out in the city, too. He knew all about the Mob from growing up around its members; but he had been brought up by a good family whose values led him to join the FBI. The FBI didn't know who he was anymore. No one named Joe Pistone was working there, nor was there one in the company records; his personnel file had been removed and his desk had been entirely cleaned out. As Pistone himself says of his old life: "I obliterated it."

While Pistone was immersing himself in Mob life, the FBI was trying to figure out who this new guy with the Bonanno family was—Pistone had remade himself into a jewel thief named Donnie Brasco.

As it turns out, Pistone was so deep that even FBI surveillance teams who were following him had no idea who they were taking pictures of. The name Donnie Brasco was suddenly everywhere, but the FBI didn't know where he had come from. Most wiseguys had grown up in or near the city, but Brasco's story was that he was from California and had spent time in Florida doing some jobs (i.e., burglaries) before coming here.

When Pistone was officially brought in to the Mob, it was by Benjamin "Lefty Guns" Ruggiero. That day, he became a "connected guy"—someone connected to the Mob—but not officially a "made guy" (or wiseguy), which is an official member of Cosa Nostra. But you don't just get connected to the Mob that easily. Pistone had spent more than six months working undercover in New York, becoming a regular at Carmello's, before he could gain Ruggiero's trust. It was this patience, this diligence, that helped him move quickly up the ranks.

His first moves, though, were subtle ones. At Carmello's, he would occasionally see mobsters the FBI wanted more information about, but, as he said, "I never got an opportunity to get into conversation with them. It isn't wise to say to the bartender, 'Who is that over there? Isn't that so-and-so?' " Pistone "wanted to be known as a guy who didn't ask too many questions, didn't appear to be too curious. With the guys we were after, it was tough to break in. A wrong move—even if you're just on the fringes of things—will turn them off." Instead, Donnie Brasco learned to play backgammon (a game wiseguys played a lot around then) and just hung out. Around Christmas, he was able to get into a couple of games with the right people. He introduced himself as "Don," and let people see him hanging around so they would recognize him as a regular at the bar. Now he could sit around and chat with the others.

"What do you do?" asked Marty, the bartender, eventually. Marty wasn't a Mob guy, but he knew that many of his clientele were mobsters. That kind of question wasn't "the kind you answer directly," claims Pistone. So he said, "Oh, you know, not doing anything right now, you know, hanging out, looking around. . . . Basically, I do anything where I can make a fast buck." He made clear what kind of guy Donnie Brasco was, and word got around. In Pistone's own words,

> The important thing here in the beginning was not so much to get hooked up with anybody in particular and get action going right away. The important thing was to have a hangout, a good backup, for credibility. When I went other places, I could say, "I been hanging out at that place for four or five months." And they could check it out. The guys that had been hanging around in this place would say, "Yeah, Don Brasco has been coming in here for quite a while, and he seems all right, never tried to pull anything on us." That's the way you build up who you are, little by little, never moving too fast, never taking too big a bite at one time. There are

occasions where you suddenly have to take a big step or a big chance. Those come later.

Finally, the time was right for Pistone to make a move. He brought some jewelry from the FBI that had been confiscated during investigations to the bar with the intention of selling it to the mobsters. Since cops are always trying to buy illegal items, to make a bust, Brasco decided he would do something different. Because he had already made clear to anyone who asked that Brasco wasn't on the up-and-up, he could try to sell "a couple of diamond rings, a couple of loose stones, and a couple of men's and ladies' wristwatches" to the bartender. Pistone recounts the story:

"If you'd like to hold on to these for a couple days," I said, "you can try to get rid of them."

"What's the deal?" he asked.

"I need $2,500 total. Anything over that is yours."

And so it began. At Carmello's, he met Albert, who was connected to the Colombo family; from there, he hooked up with Jilly's crew, which stole all sorts of goods around New York and sold it in a place called Acerg (backward for Jilly's last name, Greca). From there, he connected with Tony Mirra, a soldier for the Bonanno family. Mirra was a knife man, and Brasco was told, "If you ever get into an argument with him, make sure you stay an arm's length away, because he will stick you."

Today, Pistone lives under an assumed name somewhere in the United States with his family. He stayed in the Mafia for six years and was so deeply immersed in that life that, at one point, he was one kill away from being made—turned into a real mobster. He claims that the whole time he never lost his moral compass, never doubted himself or strayed from his mission. He brought the Mafia to its knees; every individual the FBI would go after during this time, it would get—all because of Pistone, the best infiltrator ever to have entered the Mob. La Cosa Nostra never truly recovered.

There's a lot we could learn from Pistone's efforts, but first, we'd like to introduce you to another imposter of a wholly different variety: Alan Conway.

Stanley Kubrick

Who was Alan Conway? Videos display him as an older British gentleman, effete and smug, with a sparkle in his eye and gray hair. But Conway is in fact much more than that. He is a small-time British con artist who became famous for impersonating Stanley Kubrick in the early 1990s. It was an act he kept up despite many challenges—namely, that he looked nothing like Kubrick. The famous director had dark, deep-set eyes, was famous for his thick beard, was of a different nationality and a different accent than Conway. In addition, Conway barely knew anything about the famous film director's movies.

Despite this, Conway had conned many, many people. One was well-known *New York Times* columnist Frank Rich, who was in London in 1993 and, with three other journalists, met Conway at a club. Although Rich had met Stanley Kubrick before, it didn't prevent him from being duped. ("I shaved my beard off," Conway told him.) Rich wrote about his meeting with the Kubrick imposter in the *Times* shortly thereafter. He said of the incident:

> On our euphoric way out, we quizzed the manager [of the club], who knew only one member of the group Conway was with: a white-haired man, whom he said was a Conservative Member of [British] Parliament.

"That . . . should have been the tip-off," a friend at The Associated Press told me when commiserating two days later. "They're always surrounded by con men and rent-boys."

By then, an executive at Warner Brothers who had been reached by phone had expressed his delight at the news that a tableful of journalists had been duped. He also told us that Kubrick's new film was no secret, but was in fact a well-publicized adaptation of a novel by someone I know. Kubrick's assistant called to add that the director was neither beardless nor gay but was concerned about the impostor, who had been sighted 15 to 20 times over the past two to three years.

Despite his concern, Kubrick was also fascinated by the idea of an imposter. But the director of *Dr. Strangelove*, and *2001: A Space Odyssey* was a recluse, and this is what gave Conway his strength. Kubrick had become a kind of spirit whose name he could evoke to cause others to lose control over their senses. Thinking that they were faced with the opportunity of a lifetime, Conway's victims wanted so badly to believe the ruse that all the contradictory evidence meant nothing to them. Conway was able to get away with anything—under Kubrick's name, he cosigned a loan for a gay club in Soho, for example—and was long gone by the time his victims knew what was going on. Worse, no one wanted to testify against him, because they would expose themselves as having been duped by a con man. They would be ridiculed, they reasoned, so all declined.

Conway continued his Stanley Kubrick impersonation for many years. Eventually, he dropped it and later joined Alcoholics Anonymous; yet even there he told everyone another whole set of tall tales, involving businesses in the Cayman Islands and an otherwise exciting life, recounted in a diary found after his death in 1998.

But by then the world was being transformed. The Internet was expanding in full force, and Google had just been founded, changing the way we would all interact, and who we would trust, forever.

Why Is This Important?

While most people don't know of Joe Pistone, they do recognize the name "Donnie Brasco," because he was portrayed by Johnny Depp in the 1997 film of the same name. Likewise, most people haven't heard of Alan Conway, though his story is so unusual it is unlikely you'll ever forget it.

This book is about trust; but it's also about how technology can influence it. This book is about the crossroads between the two and how that impacts your business. Pistone and Conway were able to deceive everyone they met, because, back then, you couldn't just type "Stanley Kubrick" into Google Images and find a picture of him. Conway delighted in the fact that finding information about Kubrick involved hours of vigorous research—something that few were willing to do. Today, Pistone may have had a Facebook or a MySpace page before going undercover or, at the very least, would have shown up in a few pictures on Flickr or on a birthday video on YouTube. And once your traces are on the Web, they're there forever.

What Is the Truth, Anyway?

The way people use the Web is constantly changing. People have become more wary of where the information they receive comes from, and with good reason. We read articles about how the person beside us at the bar ordering the Miller Genuine Draft is actually a paid "buzz generator." We read product reviews on the Web, believing that they are a reflection of what the reviewers think of the product—only to find out that products returning a higher cut of the profits are always rated higher than products that are perhaps superior in quality. We know how less-than-honest advertisers and marketers work to influence us. We realize that those few lazy reporters in our media who just report on whatever a PR firm tells them without follow-up offer poor reporting. We are living in an age where the collapse of 2008 and 2009 shook our trust in our entire financial system, compromised the viability of our retirement funds, and sent massive waves of distrust through London, New York, and beyond.

It is unclear in an age in which technologies such as Google prevail over almost all information whether either of the two gentlemen discussed earlier would have been able to pass as the people they did for so long. Conway's elaborate Stanley Kubrick impersonation was eventually discovered as a fraud and exposed on television in a series called *The Lying Game*; by that time, he had already borrowed tens of thousands of dollars from people who believed him to be the real thing. As for Joe Pistone, his true identity was never exposed (that is to say, until the FBI revealed it). This enabled him to eventually send more than 100 members of the New York Mob to prison, striking a serious blow to the Mafia. How would he have done this in the twenty-first century, with much of our communication going through digital channels? Obliterating an identity online as well as in the real world is extremely difficult.

It's difficult to reach out and do business with people using the Web. This is especially true in an environment where trust isn't previously established and where the prospective customer has access to far more information about your organization, products, and services than ever before.

How Humans Shape the Web

Although the general public's level of mistrust is at an all-time high, there are individuals and companies who do successfully use the Internet to establish levels of trust in the communities where they operate. In the technology sector, a person such as Robert Scoble (circa Microsoft days) stands out as someone who, by the nature of how he communicated about his formerly faceless company, developed a strong level of trust among his online community. In the United Kingdom, JP Rangaswami is managing director of BT Design for BT Group. His blog, Confused of Calcutta, is often about cricket, music, food, and many things not related to a major telecommunications company; yet, because of his stories and conversational writing tone, we trust Rangaswami and have a positive opinion about BT.

Those who are most familiar with the digital space—we refer to them as "digital natives"—have become accustomed to a new level of transparency. They operate under the assumption that everything they do will eventually be known online. Realizing they are unable to hide anything, they choose not to try. Instead, they leverage the way the Web connects us and ties our information together to help turn transparency into an asset for doing business.

Transparency

You probably know what we are about to tell you, but it's possible you've never much thought about it. For every photo that a magazine uses as part of an article, there are perhaps another 60 that won't be used. For every quote a journalist pulls from a source for a story, there are several minutes of conversation that weren't used. This is simply editing, and a part of storytelling. Except for when it isn't.

What if there are times when we want every possible angle, every possible description, every version of the story that we can get our hands on? What if what was left on the cutting room floor is of real value to the public? Think about moments of world-impacting news, or even moments within your company where a rumor leaks into the mainstream. It is those hidden moments, the forgotten photos, the deleted details that tell the true story.

We are in a new era of increasing transparency, and it is becoming obvious from a number of angles that the world will never be the same because of it. Information flows faster and is everywhere. Human memory is slowly becoming obsolete. We barely need to remember everyone's name continuously when all of their information is all over the Web; it's all in public view. Clay Shirky examines this phenomenon in his book, *Here Comes Everybody*, in which he explains how the barriers that have prevented like-minded individuals from coming together are disappearing, allowing us all to transmit our thoughts and get information faster than we ever could before.

Because of this, secrets are now also becoming obsolete. First, digital photography made everyone look like a supermodel online. (It's easy to look great when you choose the best of 100 photos.) But then, something else happened. People gained the ability to upload their own pictures, the ability to tag themselves (affix information about themselves) to other people's pictures; and they put all of this online. The next thing you know, all those terrible pictures of you—including the unflattering ones a photographer would have selectively edited and removed—are all over the Web. If you extrapolate forward from bad pictures of you to potential corporate scandal, or even to something as simple yet life-altering as how your online profile impacts a company's interest in hiring you, the picture (pimples and all) becomes even clearer.

Those who are active on the Web now realize that they need to embrace this new transparency, that all things will now eventually be known. Companies can no longer hide behind a veneer of a shiny branding campaign, because customers are one Google search away from the truth. Further, they join activist groups to stay informed about new practices, so they are often one step ahead of the people trying to profit from them.

Companies must acknowledge that they are as naked on the Web as individuals are. This shouldn't be a surprise; any new medium you jump into changes the way you are seen. But since the Web is active 24/7 and has cameras on all angles, it's difficult for anyone to hide. We propose a different solution. But first, we need to equip you with some tools.

ACTION: Build a Listening Station

Here are a few free and inexpensive tools to help you start to see how people on the Web view you, your company, your products, your services, and your competitors. Use these tools, and use them as a way to understand why someone might choose to trust you—or not.

Start by opening a Web browser, and do the following:

1. If you do not already have one, set up a Gmail account at www.gmail.com. This allows you access to all the various free Google applications. (We like to call accounts like these "passports," because they let you open many tools.)
2. Go to www.google.com/reader. This will become your listening station.

(*continued*)

(*continued*)

3. Go to www.technorati.com. Type your name, in quotes, into the search bar.

4. When the results page comes up, right-click on the little orange RSS button, which looks like this:

and select Copy-Link Location.

5. Go back to Google Reader, click the blue plus button (+), and paste what you copied into there (either right-click paste or use CTRL-V for Windows, CMD-V for Macs).

Repeat these steps for as many different terms as you might want to search for (your company, your product, your competitors).

For the bonus round, go to http://blogsearch.google.com and do the same searches. Then go to http://search.twitter.com and search there, too. Add all these things back into your listening post, and search for other ways to do the same thing. Are you likely to show up on YouTube? Do a search there. Anything new come out that we haven't mentioned? Check there, too.

If you end up with too much in one big pile, Google Reader allows you to build folders. You can start out by labeling one "me" and one "them." It might help you sort.

How Trust Is Modified by Media

Imagine that the radio had been invented yesterday. Suddenly, you and everyone you know hears about this machine, and one day, you actually see one at a local breakfast place. Picture it: For the first time, you are hearing music coming out of a machine instead of being played live right before you. Or perhaps, if you couldn't afford to see a band play live, you were able to hear music for the first time. What now?

At this moment, something incredible is happening. If you are open to new ideas, you may simply think about how amazing this is. Now imagine that, following this song (we imagine a really jazzy Benny Goodman number), you hear a news broadcast.

Think about it. What happens? You're hearing a human voice right next to you, as if it's speaking directly to you. Some questions would pop up: Who is this person? Should you trust them? How true is this information? The answers would have a lot to do with the information being broadcast, as well as the sincerity and timbre of the person's voice. A variety of factors come into play, all of which will cause you to wonder what's going on. If you need something concrete, consider two extreme examples of this: Imagine the Hindenburg disaster (*"Oh, the humanity!"*), and then think about the famous *War of the Worlds* broadcast, directed by Orson Welles. How would you react?

Whether you imagine yourself to be trustworthy or not, one thing remains true: The medium has transformed the message. An official-sounding voice might make you confident that what you're hearing is true. Another voice might give you the impression that it's a radio drama, fiction being performed for you through the technology in this new box.

This book is about all the new radios being invented in our day, from the common ones like Web pages, e-mail, or instant messaging, to the newest: YouTube, Twitter, and beyond. In our radio example, someone had to take control to get that broadcast to you. Likewise, there are people out there right now working to understand these new technologies and learning everything about how to use them—from etiquette to audience building and beyond. They are learning the ropes. They are the pioneers, mastering the latest one-to-many communications methods. Like your kids, they know more about technology, and maybe even more about people, than you do; and that makes them very powerful.

We call them *trust agents*.

Why Trust Agents, and Why Now?

Who we trust has changed. We know from personal experience that this generation and the next aren't blindly trusting information from just any random source. In fact, upon conducting research in this field, IBM discovered that 71 percent of 18- to 24-year-olds studied spend more than two hours online per day, compared to only 48 percent of the same group who spend two hours watching television. One-third of them (32 percent) received advice about where to go on the Web mostly from friends. Consider your own behavior; you'll likely realize that your own skepticism is also on the rise.

We are currently living in a communications environment where there is a *trust deficit*. As a society, we no longer have confidence in advertising. We are hostile to those who appear to have ulterior motives, even if they're just selling themselves. The result is our tendency to join together into loose networks, or tribes, that gather based on common interest. We are suspicious of anything that comes to us from outside our circle of friends. We form groups of like-minded individuals around those topics, products, or news items that interest us. For example, the news-sharing site Digg.com reports news quite differently than Reddit.com, the *London Times*, or the *Wall Street Journal*. And that news might be suspect in certain circles, because the stories on Digg that reach the top are sometimes moved to the top by dubious means: voting campaigns, robotic algorithms, and so forth. Again, we ask you: Whom should you trust?

Trust agents have established themselves as being non-sales-oriented, non-high-pressure marketers. Instead, they are digital natives using the Web to be genuine and to humanize their business. They're interested in people (prospective customers, employees, colleagues, and more), and they have realized that these tools that enable more unique, robust communication also allow more business opportunities for everyone.

Who, exactly, are trust agents? They are the power users of the new tools of the Web, educated more by way of their own experiences and experiments than from the core of their professional experiences. They speak online technology fluently. They learn by trying, so they are bold in their efforts to try on new applications and devices. They recommend more, and more often, on social bookmarking applications (Delicious.com and the like) than anyone else. They connect with more people than anyone else, and they know how to leave a good impression. As they do so, they build healthy, honest relationships. Trust agents use today's Web tools to spread their influence faster, wider, and deeper than a typical company's PR or marketing department might be capable of achieving, and with more genuine interest in people, too.

We need to become them—and to harness them.

As we delve more deeply into this topic, we intend for you to consider two things: (1) how to be genuine, real, and open with people while also (2) recognizing that if you can think strategically and understand certain principles, you can learn how to master tomorrow's radios as well as trust agents do. You can bring the news to people. You can build influence, share influence, and benefit from the other currencies that such exchanges of trust deliver to you.

Most people will do this within a business setting while working for a company, but always with an eye toward being legitimate and honest with the community within which they operate. The more you read, the more you'll realize that we're asking you to balance being genuinely part of an online community with being aware of business opportunities, and how executing the trust agent's strategy can realize business goals. We know that this can be tricky business, but also that it's absolutely possible. Further, we believe you can do it, too.

A Trust Agent's Version of a Resume or CV

We know that you hate your resume; hey, we hate resumes, too. They don't really represent us. They diminish our skills and demean the complexity of our experiences. For almost every job that we've held in the past three years, neither of us has had to present a resume, ever. We want you to get the job you want *without* a resume. This book will teach you how. As you build up social capital and reputation, don't forget to create a spectacular "About" page on your blog. Weight it heavily toward what others might hire you to do or how they might partner. Remember that this counts internally as well.

The Web is such a powerful resource for leveraging contacts and presenting our strengths that a curriculum vitae (CV) becomes irrelevant. It's not so much that you won't need one, but that you'll never be asked for a CV because your reputation will precede you. Instead, you'll just get hired. Read on.

The Matrix Thing

When discussing the core concepts of trust agents, we find ourselves thinking a lot about the concepts in the movie, *The Matrix*—the first one, not the others. If you've seen it, you know that Morpheus shows Neo that the life he's lived up until that point was all a big program. Neo learned that if he could figure out the program and navigate the space outside of the world, then he could figure out and "own" the Matrix, which is to say, ignore what everybody else sees as rules or laws. Well, that's kind of what we're talking about.

There is a lot of similarity in realizing the inherent game-like structure of online interactions; and there are some similar (and some different) methods in which we choose to interact with these experiences. We believe in the value of people and in being genuine with them. At the same time, we also realize that people frequently act within the context of these structures, and that if we want to find a way to success, it often involves breaking our connection to that structure.

There are two ways to proceed with doing business: One is to work completely within the system and to operate by the natural rules that exist. The other is to realize its structure, understand the rules that dictate the functions of the system, and to then choose whether to work strictly within it or not—or even to move between different systems that might get you to a goal better (sooner, faster, cheaper, etc.). In researching this book and organizing our thoughts on how we interact with people on the Web, we realized that there's a big difference between those who play strictly within a system and those who work outside it. We tend toward the latter, and you can, too. But we'll explain more about that later.

Beyond that, you don't have to know much about the Matrix to enjoy the rest of the book. We promise.

Media and What They Do

We all know what the word *media* means, but in his 1964 book, *Understanding Media: The Extensions of Man* (from which comes the famous slogan, "The medium is the message"), author Marshall McLuhan describes a medium as any extension of the human body. We like to think of media in the same way.

By expanding our ideas of what a medium is to McLuhan's definition, we come to see that wheels are a medium, because they are extensions of our feet, and that money is a medium that extends human power. It follows that we view online social networks (the Facebooks and Twitters of our time) as media, not because they help us communicate, but because they *extend human relationships*. This is something that neither television nor radio ever could have done, because they were all *one-way*. E-mail never did it as effectively, either, because the communication didn't occur in a public space. Now, with the advent of blogs, our communications can reach everyone, and thus we can *connect* with everyone, because they can respond to us directly.

There's a big difference in the way traditional print, radio, and television media was used from the 1950s until present. These extensions let us blast something to everyone who had a receiving device. Newspapers, magazines, television, and radio were all different ways to interrupt people, grab their attention, and shove a message into their thought processes. In the case of television, and during the heyday of print advertising, something interesting was happening: the mix of it being a novelty (not everyone had a TV, so conversations were often about every detail and nuance of the experience) and being persuasive before we had tools to counter any of the claims (a few scant years earlier, the radio drama, *War of the Worlds*, was mistaken as being a true news report of an alien invasion). This has changed over the past number of years, and even more powerfully in the past few (from around 2001 until the present).

Somewhere along the line, institutions took ownership of certain media. Newspapers won't print anything you send them. Televisions won't play the video you made, and radio doesn't always play the songs you want or read the news you feel is important.

Over the past year, all of these systems have met with competition from an entirely unexpected source: you. You can print anything you want on your blog. You can post any video you want on YouTube, Blip.tv, or several other services. You can make your own music and share it; you can podcast whatever appeals to you. Because of this, McLuhan's true vision of media as an extension of ourselves is truer than ever. We've chosen to make the next media *ours*, and we've shaped our own media to be an extension of our own views, our own businesses, and our tribes.

We see now why this is an important time and why the communicators of today need a new title: that of *trust agent*.

Why Trust Agents?

Having learned about the rainbow while we were growing up, almost any of us could easily recite its spectrum of colors without a problem: red, orange, yellow, green, blue, indigo, and violet. But were you aware that at least one of these—orange, a color we take for granted—did not always exist? In fact, its first official use was recorded in the court of Henry VIII. No one used the term before the actual fruit (the orange) arrived from China in the tenth century. We call people *redheads* and use the term *goldfish* because *orange* didn't exist back then.

New terms, in fact, are invented all the time and thus shouldn't really surprise anyone. *Podcast*, a word that describes audio that you subscribe to over the Internet, became the *Oxford American Dictionary*'s Word of the Year in 2004 and is now so common that many of us on the Web don't think twice before using it. Likewise, *trolling*, the act of anonymously annoying the hell out of people over the Internet, is another recently coined term. There is a vernacular here that is at once common to people online and foreign to those from other cultures, similar to the esoteric language used by Harley riders, Manchester football fans, or wine enthusiasts.

Trust agent isn't the kind of thing you would call yourself. That's like people calling themselves gurus, divas, goddesses, or experts. Let other people call you that. We prefer to say "trust agent moves" and point out people who act as trust agents. For example, we'll say, "It's cool how Gia Lyons made that reference to Mzinga and Awareness. What a trust agent move." (In this case, by praising her competitors, we recognize that Gia is building our trust in her own perspective, and her own company.)

In another sense, "trust agent" can be a kind of unofficial job title. Some of these people have roles like "community manager," or they might be in the online-facing part of "public relations." The name isn't synonymous with either title. First, communities don't want to be managed: They want to be *cared for*. Second, public relations departments fill people's e-mail inbox with dozens of cold pitches every day (we've even received offers for free sneakers by e-mail in exchange for blog posts). That said, we promise we're not here to trash PR professionals—at least not the good ones.

You'll get a hang for who trust agents are, and you'll learn what being a trust agent entails. People who humanize the Web are trust agents. People who understand the systems and how to make their own game are trust agents. People who connect and build fluid relationships are trust agents. By the end of this book, you'll probably be a trust agent, too. Just don't call yourself one.

The Basics: Social Capital

In October of 2002, after the largest study on humor ever conducted, scientists discovered what they believed to be the funniest joke of all time. Conducted over the Web, the study collected more than 40,000 jokes and attracted almost 2 million ratings. This was the winning joke:

> Two hunters are out in the woods when one of them collapses. He doesn't seem to be breathing and his eyes are glazed. The other guy whips out his phone and calls the emergency services. He gasps: "My friend is dead! What can I do?" The operator says: "Calm down, I can help. First, let's make sure he's dead." There is a silence, then a shot is heard. Back on the phone, the guy says: "Okay, now what?"

The beauty of a joke (and information of many varieties) is that it can be infinitely reused without losing any of its value. But there's more at work here. You may not have realized what just happened, so we'd like to play it back to you, in slow motion, step by step.

First, we decided to include a joke at the beginning of this section. We didn't invent it; in fact, it was submitted by psychiatrist Gurpal Gosall, from Manchester, United Kingdom, to the aforementioned study. What happens then? Well, you read the joke, and if we did our job right, you laughed. However, it's what happens afterward that is interesting; but before we explain that, consider the next example.

Chris has an apple, and Julien has a dollar. Let's say that Julien wants an apple and that Chris would rather have a dollar than a piece of fruit, so they decide to trade. Simple, right? At the beginning of this story, Chris had an apple and now he has a dollar. We can actually continue to follow this dollar on its journey if we like, being traded for apples the world over, but the point is made: That is, dollars don't just grow on trees. They don't simply duplicate by being passed around. They are exchanged for goods. That's it.

What about our joke? Let's say you take our joke and tell your friend. What happens? Hopefully, he or she laughs, and then you both have the joke. It isn't gone; both you and your friend have it. When we follow the joke along its path, though, something remarkable happens. Everyone is left just a little bit richer. Not only did they laugh, but now they can tell it as well.

Our joke is an example of social capital. *Capital* is usually defined as "any form of wealth capable of being employed in the production of more wealth." Our joke has value; it's hard to nail down exactly what the value is, but it's clearly there. Therefore, it is a form a wealth, just as in our definition. But our joke isn't regular capital—you can't put it in a savings account and you can't (usually) trade it for an apple. So, what is it?

In this way, *social capital* is different from other kinds of capital. When people come together and share a meal, they not only end up fed, they also become tighter as a group. The mere act of gathering means that they will exchange things—stories, favors, and laughs—and will grow richer as a result. It may sound touchy-feely, but these things have real value. And we don't just mean that they keep you warm on a cold winter night, either; we mean they have real value, as in "you can take it to the bank" value. But how?

It's simple: Jokes aren't the only form of social capital; favors are, too. Buying somebody a cup of coffee is a real exchange of value, and it can at some point be repaid. You can never truly be sure *how*, but the fact that it can be repaid is unquestionable: You can ask for that cup of coffee back one day. Just think of your favorite television cop drama and how often the phrase "you owe me a favor" is uttered. These things are real.

We've already made clear that social capital has real value; if you find someone a job, then that person may find a job for you when you really need one. The real magic—the core of our argument—is what happens on the Web. Because the Web is made out of text, everything on the Web is written down, and once it's out there, thanks to Google, it will always be out there. This brings us to something we call *putting it on paper*. And it will change the way you think of our basic joke forever.

Putting It on Paper

What happens when we put our joke on our Web site or on our blog? At first glance, it shouldn't be much different than telling friends. But in fact, it is extremely different; it is much more powerful and long lasting. And the reasons may surprise you.

Publishing our joke to a recent blog post may allow it to be seen by only a dozen visitors, or it may be seen by hundreds. In that way, this isn't very different than telling a joke in a bar, or maybe getting onstage and doing stand-up at an open-mike night. The difference between putting it on the Web (or in a book, for that matter) is that when the joke is being told on the Internet, the joke teller *is no longer there*. The joke teller is gone. Yes, the joke is still being told, and yes, the teller is still getting credit for it. He or she is still participating, but that participation is no longer active.

The same is true of YouTube. When the famous *Evolution of Dance* video was first posted on YouTube (by our count, in April of 2006), the video's originator, Judson Laipply, may have been present to upload it. Obviously, he was also there when he performed it. But after it went viral on the video-sharing site—eventually reaching a view count of more than 98 million views at the time of this writing—Judson Laipply was not there. He may have been having lunch, going on a date, doing another stand-up act, or even *sleeping*; but his presence was being felt, in different places all over the globe, by dozens of people at a time. In some small way, despite his absence, he was participating in each of those viewings.

You may think, so what? After all, you can write a book and sell a couple of copies. Your ideas are being spread passively there, too. But you can create a book only every little while. On the Web, you are participating *all the time*.

This may seem insignificant when it comes to a joke video. After all, none of the people watching the *Evolution of Dance* are paying Laipply. What is he getting out of it? (Actually, after seeing it live onstage in Las Vegas for a private party, we have a feeling that Laipply is probably making a living dancing for private events.) But our joke is just a colorful example. If we like, we can replace it with information about a coming emergency, or we can post a blog about some important information, or, if we want to really bring the point home, we can replace our YouTube video with a good sales pitch. All of this can be doing a salesperson's job, over and over again, without that person's need to be present.

Let's compare this to our original example. Say that you read the previous joke and tell it to some friends. Though you won't be there when they retell the joke, do you think your friends will credit you as the originator of the joke when they retell it? We consider it unlikely. Jokes spread, perhaps even more virally than YouTube videos, but they are rarely credited; comedians can attest to that. But YouTube videos *are* credited. Laipply may not be getting paid for every visit to his 15 minutes of fame, but some people are paying attention to who he is. As a matter of fact, Laipply self-identifies on the video as an "inspirational come-dian." Can we really believe that he's never gotten a call about that? (After all, it is a pretty funny video.)

What are we to do when we realize that a video like this can do work for us like this? That is to say, it can tell people about who we are and convince them of our value, even when we're not there. Your authors (and many others) have realized the logical conclusion to this: Writing everything online, where it's eter-nally visible to everyone, forever, has value. Even if each video you post or each article you write convinces only a few people, that's a pretty great way to build up influence. In fact, it can make all other, non-web-based ways seem trivial. After all, we don't see Tony Robbins coaching one person at a time, do we? Instead, he works in auditoriums full of people, with all his success being seen by every one of them. He also sells tapes of them later.

The Web is like this, too, except we're not putting on a show; we're just interacting. We used to do that by e-mail, which is private; but the fact that it's all done in public view now means that all the participants on the Web are creating value for each other simultaneously, instead of the old-fashioned way of one at a time and in private.

Let's take a concrete example: Say that you're asked a question by e-mail about a specialty of yours—for instance, banking products. You could just respond by e-mail, but you don't. Instead, you write about it on your blog. You're writing the same information, but it's public. You point the person who made the original inquiry to what you wrote, so that person gets what he or she wants; but now, anyone else can see it as well. People who arrive via Google by searching for similar information can visit and post comments weeks, even months, later. Your blog post, which used to offer answers to typical questions asked by a few people, has now become a *resource*. If you're like most people, you're receiving a lot of the same questions repeatedly. But now you only respond once—and you get credit each time someone new discovers the answer.

Imagine that you do this 500 times. Over time, you've probably been asked 500 questions about your specialty; suppose you had answered them all on your blog. These 500 posts now make up a pretty hefty set of resources, with a lot of insider information and tips, and you're helping a fair number of people. As you do so, you're starting to become known for your expertise. You start to ask yourself, what might this lead to? And no wonder. You're getting e-mails now from strangers, and they're helping you learn more about your industry. Next thing you know, you may have built a fairly high profile for yourself.

This simple process is something a lot of people do accidentally. Chris, for example, never intended to become one of the world's top 100 bloggers. These things just kind of *happen* for some people. But that doesn't mean that success should happen only by accident. We're going to try to help make it available to you by *design*. The Action sidebars in this book will help show you where to start, and you can experiment from there.

ACTION: Answer Whatever Questions You're Willing to on Your Blog. Get Credit More Than Once.

Have a blog yet? (Remember, authorities don't just talk, they write.) If you don't want to customize and host and do all the heavy lifting, go to a site like www.blogger.com or www.wordpress.com to set up a blog. Give it a name that will catch attention. It might be your name, if it's intended to be very personal; or it might be a stand-alone brand that doesn't directly relate to the company. Probably the least appealing name for the blog would be something that ties it to the company directly. (The ability to choose this varies from company to company; we understand that.) Keep the following details in mind as you build your blog:

1. Always be thinking about what subjects will help you create content. Remember, you aren't talking about your home life or your cats; you're covering a topic that *you* know more about than anyone else. Make everything you write something that's helpful to other people; if those people might also be your customers, all the better.

2. Look around on Yahoo! Answers for questions you can answer about your topic. Practice writing simply, so that nonspecialists can understand you. Don't use jargon. Use stories and metaphors, and learn a bit about copywriting. (We like Copyblogger.com for this kind of thing.) Also, look at the Answers section at LinkedIn .com, and, when answering similar questions, don't be "that guy," which simply means don't talk about your own products all the time. Instead, talk about things in a way that allows other people to use the information. If competitors provide the better product, accept it! Don't pretend they don't exist.

3. Check out other blogs about your subject; see what they're talking about to see what the hot topics are.

(continued)

> (*continued*)
>
> If you have an opinion, make it known through comments on those blogs or by writing about it yourself. Always give credit for your ideas, and be humble. Commenting, by the way, is a lot easier than starting a blog, especially if you're unsure what you want to do. It also helps you write just a little bit and can help you to decide whether you want to commit a whole blog post to a subject.

The Six Characteristics of Trust Agents

In researching how we wanted to talk about trust agents and how we would impart the information to you, we've defined six overarching but interrelated behaviors that describe what a trust agent is. We realized that if we were to build the book this way, you could understand each of these actions as a separate entity and grasp the concepts better. These actions form a linked system. We believe that trust agents use all six of them, though each manifests these traits in differing degrees. As you read about them, you may notice that you can place people you know into some categories, but don't forget to consider your own strengths and work from those, too. That's likely how you'll have the most impact.

1. *Make Your Own Game*: Perhaps the first defining skill set that trust agents seem to share is their recognition of the fact that there's the established way to do things—and then there's a game-changing way to do things. This new method, which usually involves skill, experimentation, and a comfort level

with trial, error, and early failures, is how most trust agents break out of the mold and appear on our collective radar. In popular entertainment, Oprah Winfrey went from being the local TV weather reporter to a multimillion-dollar media enterprise. Though she used traditional media tools to accomplish this, when you look back on the circumstances of Winfrey's rise, you'll recognize all the various points in her career where she made her own game (against some fairly daunting odds). Put another way, making your own game is about *standing out*.

2. *One of Us*: One thing that distinguishes certain people as trust agents is the simple defining question of whether a specific community sees them as "one of us." In his early career at Microsoft, Robert Scoble blogged about the good— but, more important, the bad—Microsoft products at the time. When he shared his take on why Internet Explorer wasn't as good as Firefox, we (his audience of readers) felt that Scoble represented One of Us. We could believe what he said, because he was a member of our community, talked like us, spent time where we spent time, and seemed to be genuine and honest with us. This characteristic extends to every trust agent we identify throughout the book. In other words, being One of Us is about *belonging*.

3. *The Archimedes Effect*: You can do any and all of these six things well, but when you use your unique abilities to enhance them (using knowledge, people, technology, or time), then what you do becomes immensely powerful. We consider the Web to be one of the best tools for increasing the power of what you do, so we discuss this with you to get you started on bringing it all together and achieving your goals. It's probably already clear, but the Archimedes Effect is about *leverage*.

4. *Agent Zero*: Trust agents are at the center of wide, powerful networks. They make building relationships a priority because it's a human thing to do—long *before* any actual business requires transacting. They are people who jump at the chance to meet others online, at events, or in mixed social settings, and who then often connect these new acquaintances with other people in their personal networks. They realize the value of our networks isn't in their ability to ask for things, but in their ability to complete projects faster, find resources more easily, and reach the right people at the right time. Because having a wide network is very powerful and opens doors, Agent Zero is about developing *access*.

5. *Human Artist*: Learning how to work well with people, empower people, recognize their strengths and weaknesses, and know when to improve relationships and when to step away are all part of what a trust agent does. In business terms, these are often called *soft skills*. From our perspective, companies that aren't valuing the power of peak performers in the arena of human interpersonal skills and social interaction are companies doomed to a painful future. This is an art consisting of sciences. It's the hardest part to teach, but one of the most necessary ingredients. Being a Human Artist, in a way, is about developing *understanding*.

6. *Build an Army*: No matter how great you think you are, you can't do it all alone. When you can get a large group to collaborate, you can achieve monumental tasks that may have been previously impossible. As more people gather on social networks and elsewhere, asking each to push a little can help it become an avalanche in a way no set of tools was ever able to do before. Because the Web is so vast, and we are so small, building an army is about developing *mass*.

What Comes Next

Each chapter in the remainder of this book focuses on one of the six actions/characteristics of a trust agent. In each chapter about a specific topic, we mention the other five in regard to how they all interact. Feel free to skip ahead if something looks exciting; we won't mind.

Most important, remember that people on the Web learn best by doing and that reading this book is only a starting point. You'll need the real experience of all this to start to really understand what we mean.

Let's dig in.

2

Make Your Own Game

Poster Child?

Mario Lavandeira, circa 2004, sounds like a real winner. First, he gets fired from *Star* magazine, the gossip rag. Next, he jumps on a plane to New York to become an actor. He blows that, too. But don't cry for him just yet. He is the poster child for the power of trust agents called Make Your Own Game. While you may not know that name immediately, you might recognize Lavandeira's much more famous alter ego: Perez Hilton.

If you haven't heard of Perez Hilton, you haven't met a force of nature. Hilton's celebrity site, PerezHilton.com frequently outperforms *People* magazine, TMZ, and nearly every other celebrity-focused site on the Web. How did that happen? Lavandeira—er, Hilton—made his own game.

He's not alone. Sam Walton was running a Ben Franklin store, but the corporate entity kept getting in the way of his profits, so he started Wal-Mart. Steve Jobs and Steve Wozniak didn't think everyone wanted mainframes, so they created their own type of computer. Richard Branson does it all the time, most recently by deciding that he should make commercial space travel part of his game.

But making your own game is not just about trying to find innovative ways to improve your brand or business: It's about understanding that the tools to let you do this are at your disposal, and most of them are free.

Set Your Own Rules

No matter what industry you are in, there are very specific protocols in place. If you are an aspiring young journalist, there is a ladder you must climb to get published in a respectable newspaper or to get airtime in a decently rated TV market. If you are a rock band, you spend years shopping your demo discs around to various people, play for years in small clubs trying to catch some attention, and eventually get a record deal where most of the money is made by the record company. Maybe.

Or, by using a site like MySpace, you make your own game.

That's what the Arctic Monkeys, from Sheffield, England did. Their first album beat Oasis's record to become the fastest-selling album in the history of the United Kingdom, all by using MySpace. Arianna Huffington broke new ground when she launched the *Huffington Post*. At the time of this writing, her web site is the most popular blog on the Web. But calling the *Huffington Post* a blog is like comparing an iPhone to a rotary phone. They have similar functions, but deliver quite a different output and value. It's partially because Huffington used new and different strategies, such as giving celebrities a forum to air their political views, that few blogs are able to compete against her.

With *In Rainbows*, Radiohead band members decided they didn't need to rely on the traditional music engine to release their album. Instead, they released it on the Web using a "pay-what-you-want" strategy. Some called it a success, while others questioned the numbers. When the statistics were released in October of 2008, it was revealed that the digital, pay-what-you-want model earned more revenue for Radiohead than all sales for *Hail to the Thief*, the band's previous, physically released album. The concept had never been tried before, but 3 million digital sales later, it probably won't be the last time it is used. Trent Reznor of Nine Inch Nails has experimented with similar methods. Musician "Weird" Al Yankovic started releasing one song at a time online instead of stuffing albums together before bringing his music to the people. The Web can be used to employ this strategy, which we refer to as "gatejumping." It's what happens when you find a better way to do things while everyone else is too busy to notice.

Because the Web is a media platform, a communications platform, a vast sea of loosely joined resources, it's the perfect place to gatejump. Trust agents know this. They live in this space. They look for the games inside the game, and they find ways to win. Why wait for permission? Just do it.

ACTION: Write a Gatekeeper/Gatejumper List

One way to see things differently is to understand who currently "owns" the old games in the area you are wishing to increase your presence. These people are gatekeepers. For instance, Sotheby's might own live auctions, but eBay owns them online. In this example, eBay is the gatejumper. Your

(continued)

(*continued*)

local telephone company owns the phone lines, but Skype owns the online phone marketplace. Make a list of the old owners, the *gatekeepers*, and then the upstarts, the *gatejumpers*. Richard Branson decided to make his own commercial space travel company. Why? Why not? It's not like NASA owns space.

Here are some other gatekeepers and gatejumpers to get your ideas flowing:

Radio > podcasters

Print magazines > blogs

Bookstores > Amazon

Toyota Prius > Tesla Motors

Microsoft Office > Google Docs

Record labels > Radiohead, Nine Inch Nails, Madonna, and plenty more

Now, figure out who your gatekeepers are, and then decide which rules you can break to make yourself a gatejumper. You'll figure out that, sometimes, some rules are in place for a reason, but other times, not so much. Doing this helps give you an idea of what ideas are outdated so that you can get rid of them and see what it's like to gatejump for yourself!

Gatejumping: An Example

Before we read about Tim Ferriss, author of the best-selling *4-Hour Workweek*, we had never heard of lifestyle design and, for that matter, neither had Google. No one was searching for the phrase, and no one was interested in lifestyle design as a subject. Not knowing it existed, why would anyone go searching for information about it?

Even if you've never heard of lifestyle design before today, you can nonetheless deduce what it is; after all, you know what a lifestyle is, and you know what design is, so putting the two together isn't complicated. But it's fascinating to look back on what happened in the months after the South by Southwest conference in March of 2007, where the concept was the subject of a session, and the book's subsequent release in late April of 2007. (See Figure 2.1.)

In January of 2007, FourHourWorkweek.com had a red background, a smiling picture of Ferriss, and little else. It presented a prescient phrase: "For all the excitement, mishaps, interviews, and outrageous tips you can handle, don't miss my world-famous blog!" That inauspicious beginning was soon to change. In March, the site was redesigned, and the phrase "experiments in lifestyle design" became visible. Although the LifestyleDesign.com web site had been registered as early as 2002, the phrase started to become searched for only when the book reached the best-seller charts and the blog became more widely

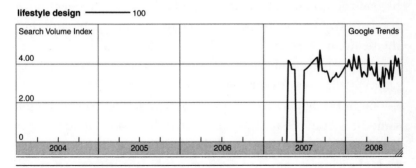

Figure 2.1 The Rise of Lifestyle Design
Source: Trends.Google.com

read. Lifestyle design had become an industry, and Tim Ferriss had become its standard-bearer.

"I wanted to sidestep the perceived limitations and reputations of both 'time management' and 'work/life balance' genres, which tend to be bland and focus on incremental improvements. The term *lifestyle design*," said Ferriss, was intended "to create a category of one where I defined the rules and set the standards. Don't be better at following the guidelines and constraints that accompany a common label—be different and call yourself such. If the concept or category you create catches a foothold, you're the first to mindshare. Let the rest of the world that follows be compared to you. Particularly in a world where power is often measured in links, this puts you in pole position."

Ferriss is correct about a number of issues. We don't want to join a race where we're forced to catch up from the very beginning. We'd prefer that everyone start at the same time, from the same position. Instead, you invent your own games all the time, in small ways—like inviting a group of people to your own local place on a Saturday night, where you're more comfortable and know all the people working there. Joe Pistone, from Chapter 1, did this all the time. In order to convince people that he had friends and a regular social life, he would frequent a bar across town for a while, get to know the people there, and then invite his new Mob friends there; by doing so, he looked as though he had regular connections everywhere, instead of the reality, which was that he appeared out of nowhere.

By not only playing a new game of your own, but naming it something else, you position yourself at the head of it, and with a little effort, you make yourself the default. Just think of Google and Googling—hard to compete with something when it's become the Kleenex or Coke of the Internet, isn't it?

What Gatejumping Has to Do with Trust

Before explaining how you can make your own game, it is important for you to understand why it should be done and how it helps build the trust that is vital to your future marketplace.

Reinventing the space you're in naturally helps you stand out. As people who stand out redefine the industry they are working in, they have an easier time making a name for themselves. The process of creating a new space for yourself helps establish you as the expert in that field, and you become trusted in the process. In some ways, the principle of making your own game works very well with the trust agent principle of "One of Us," which is described in the next chapter.

Gary Vaynerchuk is a trust agent because he sidestepped the way the mainstream was talking about wine (pretentiously), and he communicated with us on our turf using our language (Vaynerchuk tells us that certain wines have a Skittles candy flavor to them). He talks about wine the way you hear people talk about football. He created his own space, built a relationship with his community, and gave us confidence that he wouldn't steer us wrong. More about Vaynerchuk in a bit.

Robert Scoble changed the way corporate blogs operated while he was at Microsoft. He made his own game within the system when he worked with them a few years ago and created its blog, and he immediately shot to the top of the tech community's awareness because of it. But he earned our trust by being one of us. He built relationships with us. There were plenty of corporate blogs out there, but they were all the same, so he stood out.

There's an awareness element to this. It relates to getting there first, which we've talked about a few times. Being there first helps, but it isn't enough. If you're not following the rest of the principles, you will not be a gatejumper or become the defining brand in your field, and the advantages or opportunities are lost.

To better understand this concept, it's important to see the landscape with a fresh set of eyes. Let's start there.

Seeing Your Own Way

It's been said that fine-art training changes the way you see. In *Drawing on the Right Side of the Brain*, Betty Edwards describes how the process of learning to draw also changes how you see the world; you begin to see the world in light, tones, and shapes. She describes two different methods of seeing as "L-mode" and "R-mode," since they represent the different ways the two halves of the brain process information. As it turns out, when we think in L-mode, we are thinking in words and ideas (i.e., for the most part, verbally). But R-mode is different; most of us don't know how to shift into this way of thinking, but artists who have worked hard at *really looking* do it naturally. Further, Edwards thinks it can be done on purpose, allowing us to see the world more clearly without the years of training.

In our case, you need to start by seeing life as a game. This has a lot of advantages. For example, games have concrete goals and simple (usually point-based) ways of measuring what's working, whereas life does not. It is important to differentiate yourself by creating a new category for you to fit in. This also creates a new way for people to be looking at you. Much like painting can transform your vision, if you change the way you look at life and the situations you encounter, you can come to see the light and the colors. In other words, when you are looking at the painting of life, it is essential to see not only the image, but the brushstrokes as well.

How Building Trust Is Like Chess

If you've ever come across the names Gary Kasparov or Bobby Fischer in a news article, or if you've seen the movie about Fischer (*Searching for Bobby Fischer*), you probably have at least one preconception about chess that is just plain wrong: that, in order to be a good chess player, you need to be "born with it." In fact, chess is a game like any other—you learn the basic rules (how the pieces move), then study strategy in the form of openings and endgames. But you don't need to be born a chess genius to play great chess. On the contrary. László Polgár, a Hungarian chess teacher who is still alive today, can prove it.

Polgár himself is a good chess player, but by no means a grand master. He is, however, an expert in chess *theory* and is the author of *Chess: 5334 Problems, Combinations, and Games*, a book the size of a full encyclopedia, which Julien once attempted to get through. (He got as far as problem number 150.) Unlike many of us, Polgár believes that geniuses are *made*, not *born*.

Polgár is the father of three famous chess champions, collectively known as the "Polgár sisters." He brought up every single one of them at home, teaching them chess, and all became grand masters, the highest title one can achieve in chess. The middle sister, Sofia, was so good at a Rome tournament in 1989 that it came to be known as the "Sack of Rome" (after the 1527 pillaging of Rome by the mutinous armies of Charles V). Judit, the youngest of the three, is by far the best female player in history—alive or dead.

Just genetics? We think not. But what does this mean for trust agents, those of us trying to play a wholly different kind of game?

Learning from Polgár, we realize that being good is not a matter of being "born with it," but instead, follows from practice.

(continued)

(*continued*)

If chess, which is among the most strategic and competitive games in the world, can be learned, then we can do the same with our game. In fact, it should be much easier.

When you conclude that talent, though not quite a myth, is certainly overrated, you start to realize that you never need to see yourself as below anyone. Instead, you should only believe that you don't yet have the experience that person does, then find a way to get it.

The Three Methods of Games

In an article published on September 28, 2008,[1] on the popular blog BoingBoing.net, Douglas Rushkoff describes what he calls the three methods by which kids relate to games: playing, cheating, and programming. He then goes on to ascribe these methods to the way that humans generally interact with culture, as well.

First, he says, is playing. Playing is what kids do first. They turn on the computer, their PlayStation, or their Nintendo Wii and just start playing with whatever's there. They learn how the controller works. They click here or there to see what happens when they do. They try to get past a series of enemies and to finish the different levels of the game. They're playing the game as it was intended, the way the game designers made it, the way it was originally conceived to be played. If they're beginners, they learn a lot by failing, often over and over again, which is the same way we learn to ride a bike. If they're experts, they have a base of

---

[1] http://www.boingboing.net/2008/09/26/play-cheat-program.html.

knowledge that helps them learn further techniques more quickly, as in learning to drive a manual-shift car when you can already drive an automatic.

Once they've played the game for a while, gotten frustrated, or just generally become bored, kids move to what Rushkoff calls the "cheating" method. What's interesting is that these so-called cheats—codes you can use to advance—are usually built into the game; as such, they're not really considered cheating, but rather using a part of the game that most people don't know about. The most memorable of these, commonly referred to as the "Konami code" or "up, up, down, down, left, right, left, right, B, A, start," has become a pretty famous meme of its own. You use it by pressing those buttons, one after the other, on many games launched by Konami (including the most famous of the games, the original Contra for the NES). Codes like these usually give you more lives or more power-up abilities, to keep you alive longer.

Another version of cheating involves finding "walkthroughs" online, intended to guide the player through every step needed to finish—or win—the game. Again, this isn't really cheating; it's just asking for help. But it's going around the usual way of doing things; it's like asking a friend instead of finding the solution yourself. People are merely finding quicker paths to the answers they're looking for.

For these reasons, we refer to this method as *hacking*. Cheating would be more like taking another player's Monopoly money when that player isn't looking, while hacking means *finding another way around*.

After a while, this gets boring, too, so players seek to develop their own quests and build their own games. They turn into programmers. They look for tools to create alternative versions that are more fun, or challenges that are harder than the original designers ever intended them to be. Then they take these designs online and share them with a community.

What does this have to do with us? As it turns out, quite a lot. You, the reader, need to understand how to go through these stages as well—not on a Nintendo or on a computer game, but in your own life.

Very Important Point

In this chapter, we're talking about taking advantage of systems, not people. People are real, have real feelings, and always deserve respect. Always consider what's right and wrong when it comes to this stuff.

But hey, you already knew that, so we don't need to linger.

Step 1. Playing

Going back to our three-prong analogy—playing, cheating, and programming—the first thing we have to do is figure out how to play the game. All games have rules because they are representations of reality, and rules allow for all players to have equal footing at the beginning; it just wouldn't do for one person to start with double the money of the others in Monopoly, for example.

Not only are there the traditional rules of the game, the ones that are written down, there are also house rules, like the Free Parking rule. According to the various people you ask, Monopoly often has the following house rules (you probably have your own variations on these) in addition to the traditional rules:

1. Free Parking is given $500, which is placed in the middle of the board. Any taxes from cards are placed there, too. When

you land on it, you win it all, and a new $500 bill is put back on. Alternatively, free parking does nothing, or the $500 is not replaced (i.e., only the first person to land there gets it).

2. When you land on the Go square, you are given $400 instead of the original $200 for "passing Go."

3. If you roll doubles on the dice (two ones, two sixes, etc.), you get to roll again. Likewise a second time, but a third time, you go to jail.

Things like this are done generally to make a game more fun. That's a lot of what we're talking about—first we learn the rules, and then we figure out which ones are relevant to us.

ACTION: Start Figuring Out the Rules . . . *Everywhere!*

The difference between you and other people in your space is that you are going to think about the rules and systems that apply to any situation. What are the rules of work? You're supposed to arrive at a certain time. You're supposed to clock your time at your desk. You're supposed to deliver XYZ at some kind of interval, and so on. What are those rules?

Once you have the system figured out, ask yourself which rules can be ignored, changed, modified. Keep in mind, you should not break laws, cheat, or do anything illicit or immoral; rather, consider whether some of the systems that you use are inefficient. For instance, do you *really* have to be at work at a certain time? Or at all? What if you presented a case to your boss that you could work out of a coffee shop and deliver more business value? For example, you may know of a local café where all the programmers and

(continued)

(*continued*)

designers hang out. By working there instead of in your office, you can develop your network and maybe bring in new contracts. Pop! You've just shifted the rules and made your own game.

Try to find even simpler systems. How could your company improve by using Facebook or the newer social networks? What are the rules of the game? How could you hack the rules?

Playing Games Is Fun. Okay, business is business and work is work. But truly, if you don't accept this detail, that games are meant to be fun, you're probably reading the wrong book. Try Jim Collins's *Good to Great* instead. Excellent book. The rest of us, let's agree that if we can figure out a way that work can be fun, it just goes better for everyone involved. In learning how to be trust agents, we spend most of our time looking for ways to do business and make it fun. Why? Well, why would you want to do the opposite? That doesn't mean we don't like hard work. We love hard work. But finding a way to make it fun? That's the gold.

Having fun as it applies to business might manifest itself in several ways. For instance, both of us do most of our work out of coffee shops. Our office is wherever the wifi and coffee are good. Chris has done this while working for corporations, even though "working remotely" wasn't part of the original job description. Chris convinced his employers (at three different jobs and counting) that he could deliver results while working remotely—not only as good as his in-office output, but better, was what Chris promised. Upon proving this (and there were always adjustments), Chris was able to avoid commutes ranging from an hour, to twenty minutes, to most recently two hours (one way!) and do his work at a coffee shop less than a block from his house. Who made work fun? We did, because we made our own game by defining where we worked what the actual deliverable was, instead of "hours clocked in a cubicle."

You Win by Having Goals. When people get together to play, they can form fast unions, develop quick sets of rules, and play challenging and rewarding games. The games that seem to endure are those that have a goal in mind. It might be something with a score, like playing basketball. It might be something like racing bikes. It might be something a little more creative like Dungeons & Dragons or a card-based game. The games that endure are those that have goals. This is partly because of how competitive people can be. It's because people enjoy having that sense of accomplishment. It's a way to parse things into measurable segments. Books have chapters. Games have goals. Trust agents look for ways to make games, and as part of this, they put goals in place for all that they do. Sometimes the goals are written down; other times they are simple mental notes. But goals frame the process of deciding which direction to go in.

This differs dramatically from the way most people deal with life. Seeing life as a game allows you to see the map, to see where you're going. If life were a jigsaw puzzle, it would be easier, because you could see which pieces go in which area, both because of the color and because you know what the end result looks like—the picture is on the box. When you're playing life instead of just living it, you try to see the map to know how you can organize yourself better. You look for shortcuts. You can look at other players and ask yourself, "How did they do that?"

The reality is that when you look at the way most people have achieved a goal from the perspective of having completed it, *how* they did it becomes rather clear. As Michael Jordan famously said, "I'm good at basketball because I practice shooting." Sometimes it's the daily progress that most of your competitors aren't making that causes the biggest change. Having a goal helps that daily progress happen.

Some examples of goals you could set might be simple ones. In more traditional games, it might be something like, "Find the golden feather," or "Try to avoid the snakes and reach the ladders." For you, it might be, "I want to double my blog subscribers in a year." Or it might be something more specific: "I want to get 1,000 new customers based on leads from my use of Facebook." You decide. Or "I want my blog to result in invitations for me to speak at conferences." Who knows? They're your goals. But in order to be effective, they must be specific and actionable. Consider the map and the other players in the game, and see how far they've gotten. Julien does this by measuring achievement relative to age, because he finds it encouraging. "Okay, if that guy is 35 and at that level, that means I have five years to get there, so how am I going to do that? What steps should I take?" If age isn't your advantage, find something else that is. It will help you set your goal.

The Importance of (Friendly) Competition. Humans are wired for competition. It's built into our games, and it's built into our basic subconscious need, too: food, sleep, reproduction. But with our conscious brains, we take it further and extrapolate it out. Not unlike Marshall McLuhan's message that media is an extension of us, competition seems to be a driver of many of our extensions of *need*. Trust agents who develop a game mentality almost immediately hone their competitive thinking.

There are many examples of overt rivalries, of chest-thumping business owners who bark out challenges to competitors, who use all kinds of sports analogies, who talk about killing and crushing and the like. That probably works for some folks, and maybe you even have some of that motivation in your own thinking. But that's not exactly what we're talking about here.

A simple example of a friendly competition could be a desire to improve your online stats. If Chris has 25,000 subscribers to his blog, he's looking at Brian's Copyblogger.com at 49,000 and wondering how to get there. He doesn't wish Brian ill, nor does he choose a strategy to scuttle Brian's growth. However, if Chris uses Brian's numbers as a gauge and a goal, he is now actively competing by having the goal of developing a following similar to Brian's. That's the advantage of the Web: we don't need to make another team lose to win ourselves. There's plenty of room.

The source of your competition doesn't need to be external. Similar to Julien's example of age-based goals, Chris's example of competing with Brian is more a self-based goal, a goal of competing with his own numbers. Because part of game play involves knowing your score, competition seems to fall right in line with this. So, create a source of competition for yourself—maybe even only in your own head, without telling anyone. Then regularly revisit that race and see how it's going. Keep at it.

Games Have Better Feedback. One reason people get better at games faster than they get better at life is because there is better feedback given inside the game system; they can see much more quickly whether what they're doing is working. For example, when your onscreen computer game character attacks a monster with a weapon that doesn't work, it often says "miss" or makes a different sound than if the weapon were to work. This is feedback, and it's built into the game by its designers to help guide the player to victory. But much of the feedback of life and its games is more subtle, so you have to be consciously looking for it.

The Web has feedback, too, but sometimes it isn't as obvious. And unlike in a game, where all you need is your five senses (as in our preceding example), sometimes the Web will require better tools to understand what is working and what isn't. There are tools to help us get the feedback we need by providing methods to measure performance. Here are a few.

Links Links are a form of currency on the Web. When another web site provides a link to your web site or your blog post, that action tells Google (especially Google search) that what you've created has value. It's simple: Getting links means that your material has value, and it tells the various ranking systems on the Web that you're doing something worthwhile. Thus, watching who is linking and how many links your blog or web site gets is a measure of the value of your worth in a virtual form.

What's interesting about this is that links also provide indirect methods of getting paid. Let's say you speak at a conference or meet with a group of people and impress them and that they blog about you on their respective sites. Now you have not only traffic from those blogs, but a larger network being told that you and your blog are trustworthy. They see this because you are getting links from other trusted blogs. This trust helps you rise in the search engine rankings, bringing yet more people who are convinced of your expertise. It's a virtuous circle and, although very indirect, it can lead to some truly profitable business.

Comments If you're not necessarily in it for the more typical numbers, you might instead be interested in something a bit more nuanced. What do people think of your writing, your videos, or your photos? Comments are a great way to reinforce your reputation and people's trust in you. It works better if the comments are quality ones and not just "I agree!" types. As people interact with your media, they will see the comments on your media and form an impression of you. It's the "café rule." If you're looking for a good cup of coffee and some pastry, and you find a café that is always empty, you'll probably never stop there. If you see a café full of people sitting at tables, you'll probably drop in. It's social proof in action.

Sentiment There are all kinds of tools built for listening on the Web. With a little work, you can dashboard sentiment ratings. This could be anything from measuring positive versus negative mentions on the Web to measuring the levels of mention from neutral to very positive, or whatever parameters you prefer. Companies like Dell measure sentiment ratings, which is both a much more powerful way to gauge customer satisfaction and a more effective way of attracting new customers than staged survey questions, online phone reviews, and the like. Comments and blog posts and articles found "in the wild" are likely to be a more accurate reflection of a customer's opinion. You can do the same for yourself, for your business, for a product, and so on—that is, if people are talking about you.

Revenue Let's not forget that the main way a business measures itself is in dollars. There are, however, lots of ways to evaluate this. You might look at your Web presence itself as the money-maker. There are enough people earning full-time revenue from their blogs these days that it doesn't seem as crazy as it used to. There are many ways to make money directly from your blog. The simplest might be to place Google AdSense ads on your blog and count your revenue, but that's beginner stuff. There are affiliate advertising opportunities that pay per click or per action. There are old-fashioned ads that pay by cost per thousand views (CPM).

Beyond that, there are many ways to sell products and services. This method of measuring advancement in your game plan is fairly direct. Use the Web better, and get more revenue. But stopping at advertising all over a blog would be an ineffective way of reaching your goal. There are many more ways to make money from the Web (which we'll cover elsewhere).

Friends and Followers This is one way that *some* people measure their success on the Web. If I have many online connections (often termed "friends" on social network sites), I must be a great person. This is not considered a good metric of feedback. The barrier to accepting a friendship online is low. For instance, Chris is willing to accept most anyone (well, anyone who doesn't seem spammy or automated) as a friend on Twitter. On the social network sites of 2006 to 2008, there was no reason not to accept any friend requests. With some of the newer social networks, having a small, intimate, actionable list of connections seems more favorable. That's our recommendation to you. No matter whether you have lots of connections or few, don't use this as a measure of your success online.

Testing If you want to get really into it, or if you're a marketer or sales type, there are lots of tools that can help you determine how different web site designs, offers, or other variables can change the results of your Web efforts. One such tool is Google Website Optimizer. You might also check out HubSpot.com for its tool set. You can use these beyond their original intent. Perhaps your goal is to establish thought leadership, and, as part of that, you need to reach more people with your newsletter. Tools like those mentioned previously could help you determine how best to jack up your newsletter subscription list, thus giving you another type of feedback and a broader network.

Step 2. Hacking

As Wayne Gretzky once said: "I skate to where the puck is going to be, not to where it has been." We try to do the same.

When you know the rules of a system, it generally means you get better at it and can navigate it really quickly. Think of going through airport security; if you're traveling in the United States, you know to remove your shoes, belt, and watch ahead of time—that's an example of you knowing the rules and playing the game. It becomes a rote activity, very easy to perform. The status quo may be okay for some games, but for others, you may want to move further, so what's next?

Let's go back to our three methods of game play. Rushkoff's article talks about "cheating" and that aspect of game play. But we don't think this is cheating at all, so we call it *hacking* instead. Hacking is usually used by the mainstream media to bring forth imagery of illegal activities, but to the Web community, hacking is more about finding alternatives for the traditional uses of a system. An example of hacking, as we define it, would be finding a way to heat your home cheaper. The word *hacking* is commonly used because it isn't considered cheating, but rather it entails modifying the conditions of the system you are in. Let's say you're playing Monopoly with your friends. You decide that you don't have enough time to play the game as it's configured, so you make up the rule to distribute the properties right off the bat at the beginning of the game. Everyone owns property immediately. It's a work-around, because that way, it doesn't take as long to get to the end. Hacking isn't cheating. It's changing the rules or the game play and using a system in a different way than it was designed.

Hacking Video Games. One early video game example where players were able to hack the system was the fervent modification culture that sprung up around the ID software game *Castle Wolfenstein 3D*, which was quickly followed up with another game called *Doom*. These games were really popular; they were part of the first wave of first-person shooter (FPS) games, which gamers became really addicted to, prompting them to complete all levels of the game very quickly. It's what happened next that's interesting: People who knew about computers started modifying the game, adding new corridors, whole new levels, and more enemies—sometimes even modifying the enemies themselves to create newer, tougher, or just plain weirder ones.

Wolfenstein and *Doom* weren't the first video games to receive the modification (mod) treatment, but it would be difficult to point to a software game before then that had such a healthy ecosystem of *modders* (people who alter the games) creating their own levels, their own weapons, their own physics modifications, and more. This culture shifted forward into subsequent games in that same genre, including *Quake*. But by then, modification was a business unto itself. One significant example of this culture spawning entirely new games was how the video game *Half-Life* birthed a completely unique stand-alone game, *Counter-Strike*, which used the core components of *Half-Life* but changed the genre, the goals, and the game play entirely, transforming a science-fiction game into a war game.

This diversion explaining game culture and modding gives you an idea of how to look for rules within a system and then modify them to fit your own needs. In the case of modders, they did it to make their games more fun and challenging and thereby more rewarding to play. In your case, you'll probably be looking for rules so that you can gatejump them, finding a way to get through them faster.

How Building Trust Is Like Pac-Man

Among the players of the series of classic arcade games that fall under the Pac-Man banner, there are two camps: those who have mastered the traditional, original Pac-Man game and those who master its successor, Ms. Pac-Man.

The leader under the camp of the original Pac-Man is named Billy Mitchell. He played the first perfect game of Pac-Man in 1999, though he had long before mastered the game since the Pac-Man fever of the 1980s. Mitchell sports a long, carefully coiffed mullet and wears a Stars and Stripes tie—always! If there is a name that should be feared among classic video-game players, it is Mitchell's. He is considered the classic video-game champion of the world. In some games, he is literally unbeatable—by anyone.

Pac-Man is a closed system. The ghosts do the same thing every time. Master the patterns and you master the game. That's *playing* the game. This doesn't take anything away from Mitchell. He is a master at playing. Does he earn our trust? Sure, for his mastery of Pac-Man.

In the other camp, that of Ms. Pac-Man, lie other great players, a far different breed, like Abdner Bancroft Ashman of New York City. Ashman represents a whole different kind of game. In Pac-Man, you know that when starting level 2, Inky (the blue ghost) will go left, Clyde (the orange ghost) will go right, and so on. The Billy Mitchells of this world take advantage of this by analyzing whole levels in advance and developing patterns that allow them to play hundreds of levels without being caught; they even find parts of the maze where they can hide indefinitely without moving, while the ghosts roam around.

But Ms. Pac-Man is a different animal. "The prizes are arbitrary," says a Joshuah Bearman article from *Harper's* that

(*continued*)

(continued)

studied master players. You could get a cherry, worth 100 points, just as well as you could get a banana, worth 5,000. "[P]layers used to put bunches of real bananas on top of the cabinet, like a fetish, to coax their valuable digital counterparts out of the circuitry. But ultimately, chance presides: ten perfect games—all possible points all the way to Ms. Pac-Man's kill screen, at level 134—will yield ten different scores."

This is relevant to would-be trust agents because it needs to be clear: Which games are closed systems, fully understood, and which are open? An open system means we are constantly guessing and always allowing for a margin of error, which helps us improve. There are different levels of trust that come from both types of systems. Mastering a closed system means you're the best at X. Mastering methods or strategies or building a reputation and corresponding relationships around those methods means you're the best at lots of things. So, figure out your strength and apply it to the system of your choice. Be Mitchell or be Ashman—or, hey, invent a whole new category. We'd love that.

Selling the Same Thing as Everyone Else—Differently!

Imagine being told by your government (through regulations and laws) that you must sell exactly the same product as everyone else in your industry. You may not vary; you must disseminate the same information. You're held to the same pricing and cost structures. Everything must be the same. Now, imagine that you're a marketer and are told to make your product stand out. How do you do it? That's what Christopher S. Penn has been doing for years at the Student Loan Network.

Penn has made his own game by delivering nonstop value with his show, The Financial Aid Podcast. People came to trust Penn, and by "people," we mean parents (who had the money), guidance teachers at schools (who told the parents where to spend), and the students themselves (who told the parents what they learned). Whereas everyone else tried to market to their prospects, Penn delivered a nonstop flood of value by showing them how to find scholarships and offering other information to help families do more with what they had. He became a trusted resource. He showed people how to save money, how to find deals, where to get the best information; and he provided extras, like music, live concerts, and other things students would be happy to put on their iPods along with his show. All this helped him reach more people. Says Penn:

Here's the landscape, circa 2005. In the world of federal student loans, by law, pricing is set by Uncle Sam. Can't differentiate on price. There are stringent guidelines about what you can and cannot say, what claims you can make, which also restricts your ability to advertise the product creatively. The solution was to not advertise the product at all, but rather do something different.

Oh, and did I mention that in this same scenario, there's an 800-pound Goliath named Sallie Mae, whose cream cheese budget probably exceeded our entire annual budget?

This is the setup that gave rise to the Financial Aid Podcast. We had to do something different. We couldn't win on price. We couldn't outspend our competitors on advertising. So we looked for places where our competition wasn't, and one of those places was new media. It didn't take long for us to get noticed, and before we knew it, the Financial Aid Podcast had a full page of editorial content in *BusinessWeek*, visibility in the *New York Times*, *Wall Street Journal*, *Washington Post*, and much more.

Christopher Penn has delivered millions of dollars in sales to the Student Loan Network by way of his media making. His tireless efforts to move the needle in a way that maintains his relationships with his customers are remarkable. Now, in the context of "make your own game," could Penn have bought similar press in the *Wall Street Journal* (they've covered him), on CNN (ditto), *U.S. News & World Report*, *BusinessWeek*? Answer: No, he could not have bought it. Penn got his ink the brand-new way: hacking the system, finding a way around what all the other companies were doing. And the press had to chase after him to cover his success.

By the way, following press coverage is another way to know how you're doing with your own game, and it is as good a feedback system as the ones mentioned previously.

Games with Blogging

What if you knew exactly when your blog posts were going to take off and get tons of traction? What if you knew how people would receive different types of information such that you could anticipate next actions from each type of post you send? As you start to look at things as if they are games and consider your next moves as such, pay attention to the game of your blog. If your blog's business goal is to sell more widgets at your company, what types of posts do that best? Do ads on your site help you move your product, or do they just distract people? Is your audience snow blind to everything but the main content? How much do you really know about your audience and what they do on your web site?

From the way a site is designed to the way information is presented to how you write about things, you can quickly realize that all those things are levers that change the game of your blog. The choices you make should be tied directly to your goals, so don't just think about games for the sake of them.

If your goal is to establish yourself as a thought leader in your space, what should be the elements of the game? Sticking to the rules, you'd create a site showing a picture of you in a tie or a nice outfit—maybe one of those garish professional adult photos people have taken. Or perhaps you learn how to "cheat" the game and make a site where you're authentic and real and yet come off as a leader in your space. Guy Kawasaki, serial entrepreneur and investor does that with his How to Change the World (http://blog.guykawasaki.com) blog. It's most definitely about Kawasaki, and yet you get a very deep understanding of why he is a leader in his space.

If your goal is to drive sales of a product home hard, maybe you load up the site with advertisements and links to that product and hope that people click through and buy. Or maybe you're like Sam Lawrence, chief marketing officer for Jive Software, whose blog, Go Big Always (http://www.gobigalways.com), doesn't ever directly mention his product. Lawrence "cheats" and writes about the enterprise collaboration space, and when people (like us) read it, they come away realizing that Lawrence really knows his space, and maybe they should look at his product.

Another example: Chris can accurately anticipate what will happen with most every post he writes. For instance, if he writes a big list of useful, actionable things someone can do, that list will be bookmarked in Delicious.com. Then it will reach Delicious/popular (which tracks the most bookmarked items), and that will get the post to appear on Popurls.com, where it will get even more traction, like a snowball rolling downhill. Then it will shift across a few other blogs, all fed by Delicious/popular and Popurls. It works that way every time. If Chris writes a post inviting people to try out some new service, he'll receive very few comments, but the links will receive a decent number of clicks. Knowing this helps him figure out the best way to help someone, or how best to convey information, because he understands the system.

Hacking Life. An entire movement has sprung up around the notion of improving productivity and effectiveness by engaging in *life hacking*. How can you do things differently to make life go better? Examples range from ways to capture and process information, like David Allen's *Getting Things Done*, to learning how to keep your e-mail in-box empty with Merlin Mann's *Inbox Zero* Parenthacks.com. There are great web sites, such as Lifehacker .com and Parenthacks.com, and by Googling "blog," "hack," and any subject, you'll find several more. The point is simple: *Life is what you make of it*. There are rules and there are hacks. Create the game you want from life itself.

Hacking Work. This can be a bit more difficult, especially if you're an employee, but there are ways to bring this about, too. Chris comes from the world of telecommunications companies and enterprise software. Though there are probably even more rigorous cultures, a fairly standard premise of "do this because it's how we've always done it" ran through most of Chris's early jobs. Because that wasn't exactly his style, Chris sought ways to make his own game within the systems. In one case, he restored a waning departmental newsletter, which gave him an outlet to write and create art instead of doing his fairly standard job.

Hacking work requires that you keep the company's best interests in mind, that your actions focus more on ends than on the process, and that you demonstrate your accomplishments, not just your capabilities. If you're the employee and not the boss, it's often hard to strut in, announce that you're going to change the company's structures, and just start doing it your own way. And yet, there are definitely ways to make this happen.

ACTION: Starter Kit for Hacking Work

One of the toughest places to make your own game is at work, because in most places, for most people, how you spend your time is someone else's business. The first step should always be to subvert that game and make yourself more autonomous. This way, you differentiate yourself and allow people to get used to the idea that you have different rules than most people, so you are seen as outside of the system.

A lot of the time, this will involve seeing yourself as a company instead of just an employee, so you'll have to start thinking about how you can better spend the nine-to-five time you're given or how to maximize the efficiency of systems that are currently in place.

If you want to make your own game at work, here are some ways you can equip yourself for the task:

- Work for a small company; you'll be less of a number and considered more valuable than if you're employee number 5,691 out of 15,000.
- Collect case studies, blog posts, success stories, and books that show people doing something similar to what you're hoping to do.
- Win some early victories by accomplishing small projects at work. Do more than your job title asks for, then
  (continued)

(*continued*)

    surprise your bosses with it, publicly. The more you win, the more leeway they give you.

- Don't suck up. You want to be seen as equal, not inferior. But don't miss chances to subtly show those accomplishments to people who need to know. But *never* suck up.
- Find completely different verticals that do it differently. Look for synergy with what you're doing. Recommend the shift.
- Come up with a pilot program for your hacks and run it by the bosses. Don't waffle. Give them the goal, the methods, and the measures. Build a great presentation for it.

Preparation is definitely part of the game, especially if your end goal is to make your own.

What We Learned from Hacking: When It's Fun and When We Took It Too Far. Back in the 1980s, programmer Will Wright created Sim City, a game where players try to balance all the concerns and challenges of building a city from the ground up. From its early beginnings, the game was complex and challenging. You could tax your citizens a certain amount and get a sum of money into the bank for future expansion, like a real city. One of the measures of the game was keeping your citizens happy, and you'd get monthly reports on the quality of the roads, crime, and all these other factors. Essentially, the game was a balancing act of various levers. If you taxed people too much, they complained. If you taxed them too little, you couldn't repair your infrastructure. If you built too many roads, your expenses to maintain them went up, but then you'd get bigger companies and industrial complexes. Playing the game was fun.

Then we figured out how to cheat within the system. It turned out that if you cranked up the speed of game play so that years passed in a few minutes, then taxed the citizenry at the maximum amount, you could rack up 11 months of abundant money. Then, in December, slow down the speed of the game, cut taxes to zero, and wait for the year-end report. For whatever reason, dynamics in the game allowed this tactic to work. The citizens loved you. You had tons of money. And it was completely and utterly unrealistic.

By learning that trick, we essentially ruined the game for ourselves. But we also knew that we could win against anyone else. Other games did that to us in the reverse. Chris loved the video game Diablo, until he went online. It turned out that everyone else had all the cheat codes and he didn't. He was playing "clean" and they were all hacking the system. He hated it.

That's the negative of it, but there are some positives. If there are incentives tied to the games that matter—money, for instance—then learning how to (legally) make systems do what we want would be advantageous. In the continuum of playing, hacking, and programming, there are times when it's appropriate to play the game. Other times, knowing how to hack the system is important. Sometimes, the work is more involved than that. You have to move to making your own system, your own game. As you might have realized, doing this also makes you the number one person playing that game in the space.

To do this requires moving beyond modifying the existing games. It means going far beyond playing by the existing rules. To literally aspire to make your own game, the trust agent must understand the dynamics of making a game, such that there's a flow, a system, a set of rules, the opportunity for fun, and presumably a chance to be the best at that game. This is where programming comes in.

Step 3. Programming: Your Game Will Need Rules, but You Create Them

Do not go where the path may lead; go instead where there is no path and leave a trail.

—*Ralph Waldo Emerson*

When we talk about making your own game, we're not talking about anarchy or just freely wandering around. We're also not talking about literal computer programming. Simply put, making your own game refers to starting from a completely new angle with your own everything. That's the programming we mean.

When we first met, that's something we realized we had most in common. We both realized that there was a strategy at work behind our efforts, and we also both recognized how few people around us had a solid strategy. They were learning to *use* tomorrow's radios, but they weren't trying to master them or truly seeing where that would lead.

Here's a hint on what action to take to start mastering tomorrow's radios: Do something. Try something small and finite, and then larger and finite, and then complex and finite. See what comes of it. It will soon become clear that failures are just as important as victories. Nassim Nicholas Taleb, author of *The Black Swan: The Impact of the Highly Improbable* calls this process "tinkering" and for us, it's the kind of experimentation that lets us figure out what the rules of the game really are.

Tinkering is what humans do best. We all started by putting a hand on the hot burner on the stove because we didn't know any better, and we fell down the stairs because we didn't quite understand how our bodies moved or how gravity worked. But we learned. After childhood, most of us stopped tinkering; we moved into a stage of life where we felt that we now understood everything. This is the kind of arrogance that makes almost everyone believe that they know better than their peers and coworkers, that they no longer need to be making mistakes in order to learn, that they've learned enough. Unfortunately, this inhibits success.

The Importance of Tinkering. Taleb works differently: His hedge fund—named Empirica because of his obsession with empiricism—is always betting on how little its managers know. The majority of their money is made because, though they know catastrophes will eventually happen, they cannot ever anticipate them. On every day that a catastrophe doesn't happen, Empirica loses a bit of money; but on days when they do, Empirica makes millions—enough to compensate for all the other days of failure. In other words, the fund managers bet on their own ignorance. We suggest you do the same.

Start the process of tinkering. Don't put your hand on a hot burner (please), but do start a new web site, a new marketing campaign, or a new Web community. Why? The answer, you will quickly come to realize, is that, with everything you decide to do, "it's so crazy that it just might work." Understand that failure is an inevitable part of the game, but that the chance of success is much greater the more often you roll the dice. You shouldn't fear it; you should embrace it.

And don't be afraid to move between games. We don't play Monopoly forever. We don't play basketball for 10 hours straight (unless you do). Make Your Own Game could just as well be plural. Make *games*. Play poker. Shoot hoops. Eventually, you'll succeed.

About Programming. The other day Chris was listening to the radio in his car (remember radios?). The DJ played a song ("Pork and Beans" by Weezer), then played it again, but a few seconds into the next playing, he stopped the recording and jumped on the air. "Whoops," he said. "I, uh, didn't mean to do that. Or maybe I did. Maybe I was being funny. Maybe I'm being edgy like a modern day Andy Kaufman . . ." and it went on for a bit. It was a little awkward. Essentially, he was covering up for a mistake, but it dawned on Chris that this was a perfect analogy for making one's own game.

Podcasts don't have programming; radio does. Radio stations could play the same song for an hour, for a day, or whatever they want, but they have rules. On the Web, who cares? There's no law against it. There aren't as many complex forces in play (companies expecting a certain amount of airplay, royalties, etc.). Because podcasters are on the Web, because they're not asking for permission, because they don't have to follow the rules, players on the Web have an advantage. We can understand the systems, learn the rules, and then determine whether we want to hack the existing systems or create completely new ones.

You can understand that this also applies to business. Why do things the way all the other businesses are doing it? Why do your own job the way your coworkers are doing it? There is one consideration, though. Rules generally exist for a reason, and that reason is often to keep the money flowing. At first, doing your own programming will come at a cost. All gatejumping you do is thereafter a barrier to other people getting as far as you have. In our view, this means you should create your own rules as much as possible! After all, it becomes competition for the copycat behind you.

How Building Trust Is Like Capoeira

When we first heard the term *malicia*, it was in reference to an Afro-Brazilian martial arts game called *capoeira*, which Julien started playing in 2004. Though there is no perfect translation from the Portuguese word, we could describe *malicia* as trickiness, playfulness, or deceit. Along with video games, it forms the basis for what we consider to be a way of seeing life—not just as a great experience but also as a game.

Capoeira is played like this: Two players enter a circle, surrounded by all other members of the group, who either play instruments or simply observe and sing. The songs dictate the game: Certain songs indicate aggressive, fast play; others incite the players to move their bodies acrobatically, doing backflips and handstands to impress the audience. Every game has a different goal, but all contain *malicia*.

So, what is it? *Malicia*, or trickery, is a strategy to prepare your body to move left, for example, but then to move right at the last moment, so your opponent doesn't see it coming. It teaches you to not telegraph your movements (i.e., not to show your hand too early) in order to help you gain an advantage. But these movements aren't easy; you end up having to make subtle movements, without actually committing to them, that will convince your opponent. Imagine Tarzan reaching for a vine to swing from, but not actually grabbing it, because if he does, he'll start swinging and won't be able to stop.

Some of this goes back to competition. Companies keep their products and redesigns under wraps to prevent competitors from copying them, but also to intensify momentum. We're reminded of Apple before the launch of the iPhone, when the rumors of it ran so wild that no one believed there even was one.

(continued)

(*continued*)

Steve Jobs even denied that Apple would ever make such a device. This wasn't an accident. When it finally was released, it was too late for anyone to react, and the publicity was incredible—likewise the profits. While much of this comes from a fundamentally great device, it is amplified by secrecy.

While we have already mentioned that eternal secrecy on the Web is basically impossible, temporary secrecy is not. What can you do before your competitors realize they have to get in there? Think about it, and make first moves in many places. See if your competitors notice. Test them. Have a plan, and have fun.

Make Sure Your Connectors Still Work

Imagine that, one day, you stopped using Microsoft Word and started using an alternative format, like the one used by OpenOffice.org. How would you connect to those who still use Word? How do you plan for that?

Something similar happened to Julien one day when he taught himself to type using the Dvorak keyboard method. The rest of us on the planet use the regular keyboard layout, but the fastest typists use Dvorak, because it is much more efficient. Instead of the letters being placed in an arbitrary fashion on the keyboard (which is what we all use), it puts all the important letters in the middle and the rare ones on the sides, so your hands don't have to move as much. Suddenly, Julien could type faster than he ever could before, just by using the alternate layout and practicing.

Thing is, Julien still has to sometimes use regular QWERTY keyboards on other people's laptops. When he's using another computer, he has to adapt *back* to the old system. That's difficult. He used to be able to type 100 words per minute on a standard keyboard, but now he has literally forgotten how. He can only use Dvorak. It's a great advantage on his computer, but a hindrance on everyone else's.

If you're going to be doing something different, don't let this happen to you. Go off the reservation if you like, program something completely new, but make sure you can plug it back in to what the rest of the world is doing, at least in the ways that it's important.

ACTION: Three Rules for Your New Game

Here are some starter rules that we use to build your relationships online. Note: Our sentiments here are sincere. While playing the game is important, we are not saying it's okay to be fake with people. We're not. Be real, but be conscious.

1. *When you treat people well, they treat you well back.* People know that they should be nice, but how often do they follow through? The little differences add up. If you send someone a note of praise in an e-mail (or better still, a link in a blog post), it goes a hundred times deeper than what you normally do. Don't do it to get something back. Do it because you're human. But be ready to appreciate what happens when you're outwardly nice to people.
2. *The wider your network, the easier it is to get things done.* Get to know more people. Do it in person at events. Do it online by commenting on blogs. Follow more people on

(continued)

(continued)

Twitter. Expand on LinkedIn. Cultivate your network by passing information on to people who may be able to use it. We can't stress this enough: Powering your network and growing it into something far-reaching and diverse means a world of difference.

3. *The more personal the relationship, the more straightforward you can be.* As you start developing more and more online relationships, make sure that you build strong personal relationships that allow you to share genuine thoughts, not just networks of shallow contacts. Old-school networking was all about that. Stacks of business cards. We want people who will go out of their way to help each other, not just people we can ping with an e-mail. That takes work.

Why do we list the rules this way? Well, we've been told a lot of the time that it isn't easy to know what's socially appropriate or what works in a social context. Sometimes these are rules you just need to know but that nobody told you. Having a list of rules you can refer to helps. There will be more of these later.

Reinventing Wine

Does anyone at *your* wine store have a Hollywood agent? Calling Gary Vaynerchuk and his Wine Library a wine store would be like calling David Beckham a soccer player. Though he produces a video blog called Wine Library TV, it would be more reasonable to say that Vaynerchuk loves life, and wine is part of life to him.

There are plenty of wine critics in the world. Magazines and TV shows and radio shows are filled with them. There are movies about wine. Given that, how did this enthusiastic guy from New Jersey shoot past everyone else in our collective minds when it comes to what he did with Wine Library TV?

Watching Vaynerchuk convince late-night TV host Conan O'Brien to eat dirt and a cigar on live television gives you a sense of just how much of a trust agent he truly is. As part of a segment on Conan's show, Vaynerchuk showed Conan how to train one's palate to better understand the nuances of wine. Next to these wines, he had bowls of different flavors found within the wine. It was easy to get O'Brien to eat grass or taste a grapefruit. It wasn't too hard to get him to suck on a salty rock, but when Vaynerchuk crushed a cigar and mixed it with cherries, O'Brien tasted that, too. In fact, O'Brien stopped only when Vaynerchuk tried to get him to taste his sock, the one that had just been on his foot.

Vaynerchuk says:

> During this personal brand gold rush, anyone has the ability to make a name for themselves if they are true to their DNA and willing to work their face off. If you know everything there is to know about the show *Perfect Strangers*, start blogging about that and embrace it like there's no tomorrow. If you live and breathe NASCAR, that's your subject matter. The important thing is to execute against who you are; be authentic, start pumping out free content, and become part of the conversation.

What does this have to do with wine? Everything. Others might have said that something tasted like dirt, but Vaynerchuk *ate* dirt. The other wine critics played within the rules of what had already come before. Vaynerchuk jumped on the Web and mastered video blogging, and it brought him well over $50 million in sales during 2008, largely from his online efforts.

It's Vaynerchuk's ambition to buy the New York Jets football team. Given his energy, his drive, and his ability to understand the games that he currently dominates, we have no doubt he'll be successful. In the meantime, he's shown legions of small business owners and others how to take the game to another level: down to the human level and up to a place where there's almost no competition. He doesn't need pay-per-click advertising. He moves wine the old-fashioned way. He makes us want the product, and he makes us trust his opinion.

The Importance of Moving First

It's been said that the first fax machine was useless; it was expensive and bulky and, more important, you couldn't send anything to anyone. Same with the telephone, come to think of it, or Facebook, or the whole Internet.

Here's the thing: Even though you didn't think it was worth it for you to invest in that technology when it started out *then*, don't you wish you had gotten there early *now*? If you had, you might have owned pizza.com, which was recently sold for $3 million. Or you would have 10,000 followers on Twitter, just because people needed friends and you were there. The same thing happens when you move into a new neighborhood: It's cheap because the money hasn't gone there yet.

This is the same thing Warren Buffett did in late 2008. In a *New York Times* article, he stated his personal strategy in terms of when to enter a market: "Be fearful when others are greedy, and be greedy when others are fearful."

In other words, risk means reward. So move first. It isn't everything. After all, we aren't all using Wang computers. We're using Dells and Apples. Sometimes the first movement is expensive, but we like to do it most when it's cheap but not obvious.

Further, we think that those who move into a medium first set the stage for how it works, and in a lot of cases, those who come later need to follow those rules the first people have set. As we mentioned earlier with formats, and as our example of Gary Vaynerchuk showed, there's a benefit and reward to getting to a space first and making a new game. Sticking with the existing system means the same results will come forth.

We believe this relates to mastering the radios of tomorrow, too. In Chapter 1, we talked about how the pioneers of radio jumped past the media that came before it. We feel that understanding the way the Web works for business is your chance to hack the old games, program your own games, and find a whole new opportunity that drives business value home.

We recommend you dip your toe in. And more. Maybe even do a cannonball. The water might be cold sometimes, sure, but you'll get used to the cold, while your competitors will still be scared. And you'll be floating.

ACTION: A Game You Can Make Right Now

BUILD A CONTENT MARKETING BLOG

Go to an affiliate marketing site like Commission Junction (cj.com), sign up, and determine what kinds of products you could write about consistently for some length of time. Build a blog around those kinds of topics, and use affiliate advertising in conjunction with your blogging. Start measuring. Set goals (e.g., "I want to make $200 a month off the site by the second month" or "Rank on the first page of Google search for my product within three months of blogging").

(continued)

> (*continued*)
>
> See how much or how little effort you can put into each post to deliver revenue. This is a simple example of a game. You set the board. You make the rules. You decide the feedback. And then you can have fun with it. (If you're part of a larger corporation, this doesn't have to stop you. Could you build a content marketing blog around a product? Dell did with Digital Nomads, and it worked great.)

The Tic-Tac-Toe Corollary, or Now What?

Chris was talking with his daughter about games recently. She was on a web site playing Tic-Tac-Toe against the computer, and she consistently won. Chris explained that once a game is too easy, it's time to move on to a more challenging game. This relates to what we're describing here. If you get really good at the game you've been playing, and you're mastering it consistently, it might be time to look at different games, different challenges. Because the level of reward likely levels off as the challenge diminishes. Think about businesses. When Apple dominated the portable MP3 market, the stock market punished the company, citing that it had extracted as much reward as was likely to come from that sector. The same seems reasonable for understanding your own game, be that for a company or for yourself.

If the game has become too easy, maybe you need to make a new one. Or start fresh, learning the rules of a whole different game. But whatever, it's your decision. Just don't sit there. It's your move.

3

One of Us

Who Is This Geek, and Why Is He Famous?

The year is 2004. The nicest thing anyone has to say about Microsoft is that they're "The Borg" (a *Star Trek* reference, in case you're not one of us). At this very same time, Robert Scoble is wandering around the halls of Microsoft causing all kinds of havoc, and he's blogging. Not just blogging, but publicly talking smack about Microsoft, his own company, online.

This makes Scoble one of the very first (if not *the* first) trust agents ever on the World Wide Web.

Scoble wasn't just idly throwing rocks at his employers. He was blogging about serious issues Microsoft and its end users were experiencing. Scoble wrote that the Internet Explorer Web browser wasn't nearly as good as Firefox, its upstart competitor. He was right, but that didn't mean that any of us thought he would say it, especially after we saw that he didn't get fired.

Imagine this: There's a crowd of people reading his blog—all these tech geeks, business types, and Microsoft enthusiasts—and they all read Scoble's post (there were others, but this one stuck). What came next was this: People began eating up everything he said. If his very next blog post had praised Notepad as "the the best app ever," his readers probably would have said, "You're so right!" People came to trust him.

Scoble was on our side. He had proven that he was One of Us. Scoble says:

> The principle behind what I learned came out of when I helped run a variety of retail stores in the 1980s in Silicon Valley. If I told a customer that a competitor had a better selection, they often came back and said, "Can you get me the lens anyway, 'cause I like you better?"
>
> Also, people who share their knowledge about the marketplace get my business, too. I remember when I visited the "J" winery in Sonoma, California, and I asked for help planning out my day. The guy who ran the counter pulled out a map and told me where to go for the best views, best wines, and so on. I ended up buying wine from many of those places, but also went back and bought a case from them at the end of the day for making my day so awesome.
>
> I'm going to do the same thing at Rackspace, too, where I'm helping out with Building43 (http://www.building43 .com)—I'll talk about when our competitors do something great there, too.

Everything he did after that was just as innovative, and he definitely impacted the Web and its culture at large. Scoble continues to do amazing work. He is now at Rackspace doing trust agent stuff there. But this was how the game got started, and his book, *Naked Conversations*, written with Shel Israel, gave people the first and best blueprint for doing it for themselves.

Here's to you, Scoble! As for the rest of us, keep reading. There's lots to learn.

The Importance of Being Human

Gaining the trust of another requires you be competent and reliable. It also requires you to leave someone with a positive emotional impression, which is something the Web has the potential to do quickly and well. Since most of the modern Web isn't trying to complete a transaction (things like spam notwithstanding), people have a tendency to feel closer to each other there. People speak like humans on their blogs, less reserved than they would be in real life. They may end a sentence with a preposition or make spelling mistakes, but what is lost in old-form professionalism (not to be confused with lack of professionalism) is gained in bonding with the readers. Though it's a part of trust many don't take into consideration, intimacy is one of trust's most powerful elements.

As far as we're concerned, much of journalism has a faux objectivism that can't die fast enough. In the Web's new reporting and editorials, there is an emerging mass of people who are expressing their true opinions, not those scrubbed clean for an imagined audience of septuagenarians. There's real quality out there, with feeling, and it's grabbing the attention of the world. No wonder YouTube has over 5 billion videos, one for almost every human on the planet.

Within this, there is a very important lesson: Be human. You're allowed to now, in varying degrees, on the different platforms the Web makes available: Twitter for short comments you want to share, a blog for longer statements. If you need to, make whole new web sites for each new initiative. But in each, have a voice, because people are sick of brochures and sales letters. They want the real thing.

Doing this right will have an impact you will notice immediately. People will become more comfortable with you if you are openly sharing your thoughts and ideas. You won't just be perceived as a professional, you'll be a person first, and that's how you'll be treated. People will respond to you with respect, maybe even as friends, sharing thoughts that you (or your company) may never have otherwise heard, accompanied by insights your competition may never get. So listen up, but more important, speak up.

ACTION: How to Be Human

Okay, so you're afraid of feeling like a robot. We get it. Maybe you're so used to dealing with people inside of companies that you're uncomfortable with the freedom people display on the Web. No problem. Here are a few simple tips to keep in mind while you're connecting with people online.

- Remember to ask about other people—*first*. How are *you*? What are *you* doing?
- Understand the culture: Digg users are not Twitter fans. Figure out how they're different through lurking (watching) first.
- Promote others 12 times as much as you promote yourself or your company.
- Use your picture (a good one) as your avatar on your profiles on all these social sites (*never* your logo).

- If you mess up, remember the three A's: acknowledge, apologize, act.
- Share a bit of your personal life in your professional. Turns out we all like that.
- Remember that this new online world is about relationships, not campaigns. Don't just pick up and leave. (Liz Strauss* would say, "I'm not a one-link stand," and she's right!)

*http://www.successful-blog.com.

The Trust Test

Being human is important, but what else is? In the book *The Trusted Advisor*, co-authors David Maister, Charles H. Green, and Robert M. Galford came up with a formula for calculating trust in the sphere of business. "Trust," they said, "has four components, and we arrayed them in the 'trust equation.' More precisely, it is an equation for trustworthiness."

It requires a bit of $5 math, but it's worth it. It goes like this[1] (the *T*, of course, is trust, and all the other elements are what makes it happen):

$$(C \times R \times I)/S = T$$

$C =$ credibility, or the signals people send out to show that they are who they claim to be and as good as they say they are. The higher this is, the more you can trust someone.

$R =$ reliability. The more they show up on time, the more you'll trust them to do so in the future, for example.

---

[1] We took the liberty to reorganize the letters to have them spell out $(C \times R \times I)/S = T$, which is easier to remember than $T = (C \times R \times I)/S$. Hope they're cool with that.

I = intimacy, one of the most powerful emotional factors in trust. The feeling you get from individuals is important, and it shouldn't be discounted just because it's emotional. Do you feel comfortable around them? Could you tell them a secret? That's intimacy.

S = self-orientation, and this is the only negative; the higher this is, the less we tend to trust a person. An example of a low self-orientation would be someone specifically recommending a better competitor instead of themselves. An example of high self-orientation would be the smarmy, self-interested company sycophant who's always looking for a sale instead of making people feel comfortable.

When *Trusted Advisor* was published in 2001, the Web wasn't what it is today, so we will amend this formula a bit to address what goes on now. Trust on the Web is more highly impacted by what other people say. We see this in familiar systems with good reputations, such as eBay, where positive reviews of a seller's character point to reliability, despite the anonymity of those reviews. We trust the information shared by people who have been there before.[2]

Despite all the changes on the Web, the basis of trust is still the same; it's the signals that have changed. Having credibility is a major factor, but credibility is established through what other people think. Verbal intimacy is made more powerful by the lack of nonverbal social cues and the degree of intimacy shared by people who have something in common. So a lot of trust on the Web is established by *groups*, through a sense of belonging—in other words, by being One of Us.

---

[2] This works with Google, too. When trusted site A points to site B, Google sees that as a vote of confidence for site B and therefore can sometimes show it higher in its search results.

Trusting Strangers

Trusting strangers is itself a relatively new concept. It isn't built into our genes, nor are we as a species accustomed to it, but every day, we have to live it. As people have come to live in cities that become more densely populated as time go by, we have become accustomed to dealing with new faces, families, and cultures. It's become so typical that we forget it wasn't always the case.

In fact, trusting strangers has only been common practice in the past 200 years or so. Before this, trust was doled out based on who would help us survive, and, for the most part, that was based on who shared our genes. Though we still live with our families, our survival is now more complex—and often depends on the term "paycheck," instead. So, we slowly adjusted. We grew and learned to strive through the process of urbanization. And today, we depend on strangers more than ever.

The Same Side of the Wall

There's a poem called "Mending Wall"* by Robert Frost. In it, he describes what it's like to have walls between neighbors. We think it's much more important to be on the same side of the wall—on the inside.

- Being on the same side means having a customer-advocate point of view. Think from their side.

(continued)

—————————
*http://www.answers.com/topic/mending-wall.

> *(continued)*
> - It means staying focused on the relationship and how that interrelates with business.
> - It means knowing when to push back on the company should something damaging be forthcoming.
> - Speak from your community's perspective, but honor your company where you can.
> - Share everything you can while keeping your company's trust. But share everything else.
> - Stand by your community, even if that puts you at odds with your company briefly. Scoble did it, and it earned him the entire game.

(Most) Buzz Is Suspect

Here's a paradox: We trust strangers on the Internet more than we do in person. We used to be willing to listen to a complete stranger in a bar who told us that Duff's Cranberry Vodka was a great mixer with Diet Coke, until we learned that the "stranger" was a marketer paid to raise awareness. The same devices that comprise viral marketing and street-team methods of raising awareness now give us pause. How do we know what to trust?

The same is true on the Web. We don't necessarily trust buzz without a track record. Take, for example, the story of a 13-year-old boy who supposedly took his dad's credit card to pay for hookers, a tale spread widely across the Web last year. His name is Ralph Hardy from Newark, Texas, and he took one of his dad's credit cards, ordered a new one for himself, and used it to buy an Xbox, the game Halo, a motel room, and some escorts to play the game with.

Only it wasn't true. Yet we trusted it because others like us had voted for it on Digg, spread it by e-mail, or passed it around on Twitter.

The story was reported on www.money.co.uk in May of 2008, then picked up by several news sources and blogs, many of them credible. As the story was exposed, Search Engine Land's Jonathan Crossfield said, "Online marketer Lyndon Antcliff recently helped a client achieve over 1,500 inbound links in under a week with a story designed to grab attention." He went on to explain how hoax news drives people to link, which gives Google false signals of trust (see the accompanying sidebar), which in turn drives search engine rankings and traffic.

Today, the story is amended to state that it's a parody. But it isn't. It's marketing. And it worked because, despite being false, it was designed to spread naturally, through trusted connections. People love gossip, and like the new Britney Spears rumor, we didn't much care if it was true. We only cared that it was a great story.

The paradox is this: We trust strangers online more than ever before, and we're suspicious of most buzz. It turns out that in the online space, because we have only verbal cues (e.g., blogging text), we still rely on signals of trust: some mechanical (Google) and some human-based. What are some of our signals of trust?

Signals of Trust

On the Web, trust is built by a number of signals that don't necessarily exist in real life. Here are some of them and how they tend to work:

- Design: If a site looks like a basic template, without any styling or editing, we're less certain that it's trustworthy, as opposed to a well-dressed design.

(continued)

(continued)

- Longevity: Has a web site been around for a while? Have we just started reading it, or are we longtime subscribers? (The definition of a *longtime* subscriber might vary.)
- Volume of productivity: Is there a lot of content, or does it feel like someone slapped something up a day or two ago?
- Number and quality of comments: If no one's around and no one's talking, are you really a trusted part of the larger conversation?
- Number and quality of links: How did we first start reading this web site? Was it recommended by a friend, or by a site like Reddit or Digg, where users vote on a story's importance? Do we trust the recommending site?
- Domain name: We trust things from professional domain names versus "starter" domains (e.g., blogspot or wordpress .com domains are more suspect than "official" domains). We also tend to trust URLs ending in .com more than those with such endings as .info.
- Does the web site have an About page? Does it have a picture of the author?
- Does this blogger have a Twitter or Facebook profile? In other words, is the blogger interacting on the Web in several different places? Checking out what that person does everywhere tells us a lot about the blogger's real intent.

Social Benefit Occurs as a By-Product of Being a Good Citizen

One element of being considered One of Us is that the benefits or rewards you will encounter come from genuine interactions. Exchanges of kindness or transactions involving social capital tend to build on each other.

As an example, Jessica Berlin is the social media person for the Cirque du Soleil, the entertainment group known for putting on lavish shows with impressive costumes and acrobatics. Chris met her in Las Vegas at a blogging event, where she was mostly interested in meeting new people and hearing about any ideas we might have on what she was doing with her company. After a friendly conversation, during which an entire table of people got the impression that Berlin was One of Us, she thanked us and went on her merry way.

Later that night, we were at a party related to the conference. It was crowded and far too noisy. As Chris was leaving, he saw Berlin and asked where one might go in Las Vegas to escape the crush. She offered up the Cirque's nightclub, Revolution, at the Mirage hotel. With a single phone call, Berlin provided VIP treatment for well over a hundred bloggers and social media people who would never have been treated so well had there not been a previous exchange of value between Chris and Jessica Berlin earlier in the day.

The most compelling point of the story: Neither Berlin nor Chris were actively seeking benefits from any of these interactions. That's the point. This is what evolves naturally. If you act like a good citizen, and you feel like One of Us, the benefits arise without much thought. It's not the negative interaction of quid pro quo, but instead the positive concept of "good things happen to good people."

How Public Discourse Magnifies Social Capital

Getting coffee for someone is doing something nice. But get your mother-in-law some chicken soup while she's sick and she'll tell the whole family how great you are. This is what the Web does all the time, but without any one individual doing the work.

This is because all encounters in which you participate (i.e., all conversations you choose to take part in) are recorded in public (blogs, Facebook, and elsewhere) for others to see, should they be looking. You're leaving evidence of participation and good deeds to be seen by others who pass by, like markers on a trail through the forest.

Another way of looking at this is that there is a benefit to leaving a paper trail. Imagine your company is being audited, and you claim $100,000 as expenses for the year. If you have records, the IRS will believe you, but if you don't, you're in trouble, especially if you have a lot to gain. It's the same with blogs: Leave a paper trail of thoughtful comments, and you're showing that you know what you're talking about. When this is seen, it can help you develop important credibility and relationships.

Contrast this with receiving a PR pitch from an agency. Upon receiving the pitch, you search for the author's name in Google, but come up with nothing other than the agency's LinkedIn page. You search on the subject of the pitch and you see that a blogger is trashing it. You're likely to just disregard the whole thing, even if you were initially interested. Wouldn't it have been better if you had received it from someone who had met you or read about you personally beforehand, tailoring the approach to your interests?

The main lesson here is that you need to interact—frequently and regularly. Show up at events, get your name out there, but be honest about what your goal is in initiating communication. Then, if you want to pitch someone, do it cleanly and consider the reputation you've been building. This will be easy and natural, because it's something humans do naturally with people whose opinion they care about.

Half-Strangers and the Rise of "Friends"

When one user on a social network adds connections to another user on a social network, the common vernacular on most sites is that those two users are now "friends." The quotation marks indicate to us that there's a significant difference between friends who would help us move our couch and friends who might read our blog posts, buy things we're selling, or be invited to our wedding. The difference is important.

Most people have several "friends" online that they don't know much about, when you come right down to it, but then, how much do you know about the people in your office? How much do you know about your neighbors?

We proved to ourselves that there are always things you don't know about people the day before we started writing this chapter. Julien mentioned that he had a sister. Chris told him that he never knew that, and Julien replied, "Well I don't know if you have any siblings, either." We've known each other for four years by the time this is published, have collaborated on several projects, attended several conferences together, and are writing a book together, and yet we didn't know the basic head count of each other's nuclear family.

This example is typical of how trust moves around the Internet. It's something we think of as being "half-strangers." We know some things about people from our various online haunts, but we don't know other basic details. In most transactions, this doesn't matter.

Inherent in how this works toward building trust via the Web is how online communities impact our understanding of trust. If Julien introduces Chris to Austin Hill in an online social reality game (Akoha.com), Hill immediately moves some percentage of trust that he has in Julien to his perceptions of

Chris. But further, when Chris gets to know more people on the Akoha site and they start to interact in several directions (many people reaching out to other people), the community experience helps cement this new kind of half-stranger/half-friendship experience.

ACTION: How to Make Friends

Think about the real equivalent to this. Imagine going up to people at a party and saying hi. Would you immediately try to sell your product to them? Definitely not. You'd start by asking them about themselves. Same thing here.

- Online, join sites like Facebook. Find your existing friends and then branch out from there.
- It's okay to "friend" (yes, this is a verb) someone on Facebook that you haven't met (there's some controversy here, but our take is that it's okay), but if so, make sure you offer a personal message and cite the friend whom you have in common. "Hey, Austin, Julien talks about you a lot. I'd love to connect up here."
- Learn about others. In Twitter, for instance, it's easy to watch the flow of a few people to see what they're interested in. Want to find people in Twitter? Use http://search.twitter.com and look for subjects that appeal to you.
- Via blogs, go to www.technorati.com or http://blogsearch.google.com and put in topics that appeal. Use a service like Guy Kawasaki's http://www.alltop.com and find new people via his virtual magazine rack.
- Find friends along lines of mutual interests more than via geography or any other factor.

The Business Value of Friends
(and How Not to Be Scummy)

These "friends" we're discussing aren't the "move your couch" friends. They're people you know online, and you value their opinions and respect the relationship. They are humans you might never meet in the flesh, and they have allowed you into their circle(s). With that in mind, it's important to be clear about a few things:

1. Never use your friends. It might sound obvious, but people get into situations where their work as a trust agent puts them in conflict with what a friend might actually do. For instance, don't send spammy messages to friends (or even to half-strangers) just because that's what your business does.

2. If these friends are also business prospects, or potential future customers, or in any way have a business component beyond friendship, make sure to stay human about things, but also keep your business goals in mind. It's not a good idea to lose sight of either fact (being human and your business plans) during the whole thing.

3. We tend to buy from people who are like us.[3] Becoming One of Us means being dedicated to nurturing a relationship. It means being the customer advocate, and sometimes the advocate before someone is even a customer. Greg Cangialosi from Blue Sky Factory, an e-mail marketing company, was a friend long before Chris was his client, and long before Chris passed on two more sales to him. He was there, and he was One of Us. Cangialosi's company is

---

[3] http://europeanbusinessimprovements.com/Article_11_Dress.aspx.

successful despite very little marketing, because he is always around, being friendly.

Mass Microevangelism

We struggled a bit in defining the difference between a trust agent, a consumer advocate, and a brand evangelist. But we finally hit upon some big differences: First, consumer advocacy is about product or service quality, and a trust agent is about so much more than that. Trust agents care about the people in the equation. They work to grow relationships that eventually influence people's experience with an organization.

Also, trust agents aren't direct evangelists, meaning that they don't incessantly promote their own company or product. They plant seeds that bloom into evangelism on their own, through online and face-to-face interactions with individuals, through blog posts that continue to influence, or through going the extra mile for customers, or even noncustomers, because word of mouth is still more natural and powerful than any Frankenstein viral marketing people hack together.

Part of the job of trust agents is simply to create a positive impression of a brand—whether it's theirs or another's—in the mind of the customer. How that differs from branding is that they direct it to a specific segmentation of consumers instead of to the market at large, so Comcast might be one thing to America and something entirely different to the Facebook and Twitter crowd. Why? Because of Frank Eliason, who represents Comcast to a specific group, the same way a presidential candidate has multiple representatives to reach out to communities. They don't choose just anyone. Since this is common sense in the rest of the world, it can easily be applied on the Web, too.

The New Community

We used to join chess clubs and gather every week. Now we gather on Yahoo! Chess, instead. We do it every day, at all hours, because fans can gather all over the world. Players meet online and can talk strategy or just shoot the breeze—or even meet in real life.

In *Bowling Alone: The Collapse and Revival of American Community*, political scientist Robert Putnam argued that we are spending less time in neighborhood communities and, as a consequence, are losing contact with many of the people who were closest to us. The image of a lone bowler was striking, and it caught the imagination of the nation, making Putnam's book the most widely cited on the subject of social capital. But we're not sure the community is disappearing. Instead, we think it is slowly, quietly making its way online.

This momentum is based on two factors: asynchrony and interest-based locations. The latter happens when people decide to gather based on a shared interest instead of letting it up to chance and geography. For example, we used to hang out at the same corner bars every weekend, but the chances of us meeting our soul mate there is slim; the people we will meet may live close to us, but it's unlikely we will have a lot in common except for our interest in local news. Now our ability to connect isn't just based on location. Now, when we search for places to spend time, we're more likely to type "Harry Potter" into Google than "local bar," because that's what we want to talk about at that very moment.

The other factor, asynchrony, is what happens when we communicate through writing, as you would leave a note on the fridge for your spouse ("You said you'd clean the bathroom," we imagine). Instead, base it on interest. Hundreds of topics can occur at once, but without the need to go anywhere. You're sharing, and you all care about the same thing.

Wait, Is It Just Nerds in There?

No, unless you consider a nerd anyone with a computer. But then, aren't you a nerd, as well as your boss and the rest of your organization?

Maybe what you want to know instead is, aren't the people who spend a lot of time on Twitter, Facebook, and other social networks being *anti*social? In a word, the answer is no.

In the past few years, the people who have started using the Web have become closer and closer to the average person you know. The question may have been valid in 1996, but in 2009 and onward, the social aspects of the Web mean that the people interacting within these networks are interested in social activities. In fact, in a lot of cases, they talk online between in-person events and share pictures of stuff they did together.

Even the bloggers and those even deeper into it are a pretty typical bunch. We've met hundreds over the years, and we're happy to call them friends. We've played poker with them in Arizona, gone rock climbing with them in Montreal, and taken road trips all across the United States. When we get together, it's more likely that we don't talk about computers than that we do. In a lot of ways, the traditional nerd, enemy of the jock in most college 1980s movies, is disappearing. The Web is becoming full of smart, funny people whom you're going to want to know. The nerd is mostly extinct, and we're proud to count the computer-savvy, social people we now see online among our best friends. You will, too.

A Sense of Belonging

The Web has empowered a significant change in social behavior. Before the ubiquitous Web, we identified with other people along lines of geography, nationality, religion, politics, and a few other factors. If you lived in a small village far outside of London, your interactions were relegated to the people within the village. The Internet delivers ways to interact with people who share similar passions, locale be damned.

For instance, we both spend time educating others on using new media, such as podcasting, blogging, and online video. We spend time in person and online around PodCamp events or on blogs that discuss these things. Julien lives in Montreal, and Chris lives north of Boston, but that doesn't matter with the Web.

Businesses benefit from this as well. The people in your organization who are One of Us belong to a community that represents your product or service. For instance, being a Web-savvy racecar driver means that people passionate about the sport of racing can gather and share their feelings about and experiences with racing. Customer growth is not limited by geography when customers can build communities and align intentions around shared passions.

ACTION: Where Do I Belong?

Where do you belong? Are there groups of people whose ideas are aligned with your company's products or services?

Spend some time on Google searching for online communities that could benefit from using your product. Think of any search term you can and then add "community" or "network" to it. Use Google Blogsearch or Technorati to search, too. Check out Facebook and other networks to find networks of people using or in need of your products or services.

Friends as Gatekeepers

Have you ever been asked to make an introduction to a close friend, yet find yourself unwilling to do it? Or perhaps you've been on the opposite side, trying to meet someone but never quite able to connect. The human network is self-protecting, so this actually happens a lot. Because the people who are the focus of these overtures (whom we call Agent Zero types) are connected to many people and very valuable, those around them can be protective, with good reason. This happens both in interpersonal relationships and within online communities.

When you reach a certain level of notoriety on the Web, it no longer becomes possible to follow or interact with everyone who wants to interact with you. Thereafter, a sort of unwritten social contract dictates the relationship: Trust agents still spend a ton of time working on personal relationships, but they can no longer pay attention to many of them on an individual basis. Those around them become protective, and it becomes extremely difficult to reach the best people.

It's not that these people intend to distance themselves from the very people they've surrounded themselves with, but rather that they have only 24 hours in a day. When that clicks in, those closest to them act as a kind of filter.

With this in mind, if you're trying to make contact with a well-known trust agent, navigate this terrain carefully. If you have become this person, be sure to find ways to facilitate important meetings with new unknowns, because once you've cut yourself off from developing new contacts, your value to the network diminishes significantly. You must remain present to remain relevant.

The Power of Taking the First Action

Humans understand how favors work. Doing and trading favors is woven into the fabric of our culture. When people are the recipients of a favor, it's in their nature to want to pay it back. Doing nice things does make people feel good, but there's neurology behind it, too. We want to pay people back because it is in the nature of a community to do so; it keeps communities strong and protected against the outside world.

There are many questions that surround blogging and, specifically, why anyone would spend so much time working on blogs. After all, they don't pay. We all want to be paid for work that we do. The same people, paradoxically, will be glad to go to pure networking events and trade business cards to a group of self-interested people. For the purpose of clarity, here's why we blog, speak for free at Podcamp-type events, and just help people without charge: It's powerful.

The first action, or favor, in an exchange becomes a precedent that people remember. Say you are out for dinner one night and a colleague foots the tab for the whole table. What happens next? We remember that person, and we make plans to return the favor. Though it may not be dinner, the favor will be returned. We know it because that's what people do with their friends, and that's what online communities are: friends.

This may seem difficult to understand at first. How can you consider yourself friends with people you've only met once or twice, or not at all? They are not real friends . . . or are they? The definition of *friend* as it is used in this context may be different from how we view our childhood friends (as discussed earlier), but friends are, nonetheless, what these people are.

On a practical level, buying a beer for someone at a bar may lead to a second beer and, with it, a second conversation. If we were just initiating the drink for personal gain, we know people would notice. Look back at the sidebar, "Signals of Trust." People have very sophisticated bullshit sensors, and if not immediately, your intentions will be exposed later. But as long as you're not considering only the bottom line, taking the first step to initiate an interaction says to people that you want to establish a relationship, that you're interested in being involved. So step forward and take that step, over and over again. Trust us, as long as you have something to really offer, the benefit will come. We wouldn't be here if it weren't true.

How to Screw Up (and How to Fix It)

There isn't a science to being a trust agent. There are times when you may find yourself in a position where you're trying to accomplish something for your business. Sometimes, the community will reject the effort. In many cases, this means you have overstepped the boundaries of what is appropriate or what is acceptable. The boundaries, especially online, aren't always clear. Companies step on toes all the time with their online promotional efforts. It's not because companies are full of insensitive people, but rather that people have different perspectives.

When Chris co-founded PodCamp, the community unconference for new-media enthusiasts and professionals, including bloggers, podcasters, YouTubers, social networkers, and anyone curious about new media, he mentioned to the local Boston podcasters that he wanted to coordinate an event that went beyond local businesses and personalities and brought all the rock-star names in podcasting to Boston. The community pushed back and slammed Chris for making it seem like he didn't value the local figures. Chris had to apologize and explain his intention: to attract a national or international audience at the first event to change the conversation, push the education, and expand the level of interest. It took a lot of work to earn back the understanding of the local community.

In most cases, the way to fix misunderstandings and earn back respect requires asserting the appropriate combination of deference, respect, and humility. If you are genuine in your efforts, the next step after realizing that the community has pushed back is to apologize. Even if you feel you're in the right, start by saying, "I'm sorry." Next, be humble and learn what the community is teaching.

If you are the trust agent for an organization, bring this story back to the internal team. First, it serves to educate. Second, it means that you can work with the team not to make the same mistake twice. After the internal team understands what happened and everyone has agreed on how not to repeat the mistake, communicate this to the community. The most important element is a consistent stream of communication back to the "wronged" individuals in the community. This conveys a message. It says you acknowledge that you don't always know what's best, that you're fallible, but that you'll work to correct course and bring the relationship back in alignment.

How *Not* to Be One of Us (about Elitism)

One by-product of establishing yourself as a trust agent is that opportunities often arise for those who are the trusted One of Us voices within a community. For bloggers, this might mean getting free products to review (sometimes called *blogola*—look it up). For personalities within companies, this might be the strange "Web celebrity" status that leads to access to more events, meetings with big names in an industry, and the like. It's important to be wary of the potential for what we'll call an inflated sense of self-worth.

There are individuals in various segments of the online world who have risen to fame in their relative niche, have parlayed that fame into something a little higher up the social ladder, and have subsequently turned their backs on the very same community where they first gained notoriety as One of Us. The fall is almost always fast. What seems to happen most, especially with the people who transition from online media to traditional media, is that the traditional channel grows disinterested in the recently risen trust agent just around the time that the trust agent has made moves that suggest abandonment of their previous community (created through the Make Your Own Game method).

When establishing your presence online, be conscious of your own ego. This is important for an employee within an organization, for a member within a community, and for a rising star in any space. Are there ways to check this behavior? One way is to work hard at promoting others 12 times as much as you promote yourself. Be sure to promote yourself, but make certain you have a reputation for praising others in a given community. Make those around you the rock stars. Keep your head about you with regard to ego. Failure to do so leads to a quick race to the bottom for the up-and-comer.

Raising Up versus Sucking Up

Pop icon Madonna is an incredible story of personal platform building. Her business acumen is vastly underrated, but if you consider that she has kept herself relevant in an industry that typically forgets its key players by their sophomore album, it's incredible to believe that she's still drawing massive audiences (and the dollars that go with it) decades later. If you look at how she developed relationships with other celebrities (at least as observed from the outside looking in), we believe it provides an important lesson for trust agents in one particular aspect: *Raise up the newcomers instead of sucking up to the industry's top dogs.*

Early on, Madonna courted some of the bigger names in the industry. She collaborated with them; she shared brand equity to establish her own brand. In those cases, the other stars helped raise her up. Once Madonna got to the top, she immediately set about building partnerships and relationships with the newcomers, the rising stars, and the occasional new top dog. This has kept her relevant, vibrant, and engaged in the current culture in ways that exclusively hanging out with the big dogs would never accomplish. (In fact, check out how many of the older musicians are now releasing duet albums with new stars to copy this same mechanism.)

How does this translate to the online world? If you are the trust agent for a company like Pure Digital, makers of the Flip video camera (a personal favorite of ours), and you have a campaign to distribute a few hundred evaluation units, build relationships with the bloggers who may not be used to getting products to evaluate, who have smaller niche audiences, rather than simply peppering the top "influencers" with the same kind of offer. (This presumes that you, as the trust agent, have disclosed the relationship, that you've not obligated the blogger to blog about the product, and so forth. Be smart about that.)

The top influencers receive lots of offers for free merchandise. They're happy to check out new products, and they have a larger reach, but they're at the top of their game. Top influencers are less obligated to be helpful. They are inundated with competing offers for their attention. And they are already audience-saturated.

Liz Strauss, community expert and company humanizer extraordinaire is fond of saying this: "Little bloggers grow up."

The better strategy for a trust agent is to develop relationships with up-and-coming individuals in a space. The time spent developing relationships with many up-and-comers beats time spent courting the few big names.

For bloggers and other digital citizens, the same strategy holds true. If you're a trust agent, building genuine relationships with the community of up-and-comers is more beneficial than focusing on one or two big names. Be One of Us. It's easier to make the relationships work. You have more to offer. You can help the newcomers more over time, and, as they rise in their own personal success, you now have multiple allies instead of a few big names to fall back on.

ACTION: Find the Diamonds

Find the online rising stars within your industry. If you're intent on being the trust agent for the boating industry, find the boating bloggers, the boating video makers, the active forum users, and reach out to them. Ask for nothing. Just say hi, or that you liked this or that comment. Make yourself known, but don't talk about your company or business goals. (We cover that more in later chapters. See Chapter 4, "Agent Zero.")

The Currency of Comments

If you read lots of books or newspapers, or even if you've been active on the Web for a while, you may need to be reminded that the Web is a two-way medium, where people comment all the time. We do it on our own channels, with our blog or Twitter as central hubs for our ideas about life, but they aren't the only places where it's worthwhile to participate. Comments are important, too.

Being One of Us means investing time and effort in others. Employers might find this concept difficult to swallow, but this part of the strategy is vital. Others have called it "givers get." In the online world, being present and commenting on other people's work and engaging in general connectedness are just as important as any direct marketing initiatives or other traditional business strategies.

Greg Cangialosi, president and founder of Blue Sky Factory, says it best: "Have a relationship long before the sale." He pointed out that Chris and he had been friends long before Chris recommended Blue Sky Factory to his company, CrossTech Media, as a platform, and that such recommendations continue without bidding over and over. Essentially, because Cangialosi is One of Us and has established himself as such in several ways, he barely needs to do any other marketing for his company.

With the rise in popularity of blogs, the significance of comments has increased across every social web site. Now, you can comment on photos, videos, blogs, and everything in between, and with newspapers following suit, it's rare to find a place where comments aren't permitted.

However, when it comes to comments, the 1 percent rule applies. It's commonly said that of all readers of all Web content, 10 percent comment and only 1 percent are genuine content creators (e.g., bloggers). The numbers are approximations, but it is meant to show the great disparity between the number of people reading about you and the number of people writing about you— which becomes evident once you start publishing content yourself.

Due to the rarity of comments, those who comment are remarkable and are noticed. A first-time commenter is usually recognized as new, whereas a regular is often recognized for his or her regular participation in guest posts or hat tips. Because of this, being a regular commenter transforms you from an invisible presence into a real community member.

These markers of participation are important, because people reading those comments don't know whether those commenting are spending time reading your work. Just as a letter to the editor can leave an impression, so can blog comments, particularly if they're helpful, funny, or just generally useful. In some blogs, the comments can become more useful than the content.

ACTION: Make an Impact. Leave Comments, Often.

To be clear, you should not spam those who have ideas about your products and services. Here are some elements of what are considered "good" comments to leave on a blog:

- Leave your name and, if important, the company name, but don't be spammy about it.
- Comment on stories and pieces that relate to your industry, product, or service.
- Don't explicitly mention or link to your stuff, even if it's pertinent—at least for a few comments.
- Be yourself, which is to say, "be one of us."
- Make sure you're actually adding some value to the post and not just saying, "Hey, nice post."

An interesting Web service to check out in this regard is BackType (www.backtype.com). You can subscribe to people's commenting and see how others behave to guide your own efforts.

Leave 10 comments today and then 10 tomorrow, even if some are just thank-you notes. They'll quickly become a staple of your daily online activities, and reading what others have to say will help you develop your own ideas as well as leave an impression on those who follow you. You'll start to become more memorable . . . and maybe even make a few friends.

You Must *Earn Your Place* in Communities

Conn Fishburn, director of Content and Programming for Yahoo! Video has a great point about how businesses interact with communities. He suggests, "Bring wine to the picnic." Simply, too many companies attempt to jump into the fray on social networking sites like Facebook and Twitter and immediately endeavor to peddle their wares. They don't realize that we all know each other, that we recognize the new stranger in our midst, and that we are feeling marketed to long before we've been properly introduced.

It seems that since the 1950s, marketing and advertising have continued to mechanize and automate in line with the industrialization of products and services. Since we developed the ability to push out more widgets efficiently, we also decided to push out more messages in a relentlessly rising volume. Along the way, we lost the humanity and connectedness that comes with being a good salesperson. Because marketing can be measured, and because the only acceptable way numbers can go is up, marketing evolved into a much more mechanical process.

Imagine the irony, then, that this rehumanizing of the Web brings to the story. Now, with advances in technology that promote communication, we have tools that allow us to form online communities to exchange ideas and share experiences. Into this breech charge the marketers and advertisers who have followed the evolution of the 1950s into the modern day—but they do not stand a chance.

Well then, how *do* companies become One of Us? How do they earn a place?

First Steps in Engaging Communities: A Checklist

Once you have determined where your community is on the Web, or perhaps after you've built your own online presence as a meeting place for a group that doesn't yet have a place to belong, the next step is to engage a community. This community may be a loosely joined group of people with individual minds and opinions who share some common interests or passions via their own unique perspective. Yep, it's a mouthful, but it's true.

Here are five steps to help you reach into your community and learn:

1. Listening comes first. Pay attention to where people (and by "people," we mean your potential customers, perhaps your existing customers, perhaps prospects, enemies, or any other variations on your list) interact.
2. Measure the conversations. Grade them for sentiment, perhaps (e.g., "Is this forum comment a positive about our new line of chocolate pandas or is it a negative?"). Determine what counts as something good or bad. Do you count number of comments? Do you count engagement level?
3. Take small steps. The first actions you make shouldn't be intrusive. You just want the community to know you're there

and you're friendly. Create opportunities for small, memorable exchanges. Build your profile as someone known by
being around and monitoring conversations, recognizing
who's a regular and who makes decisions.
4. Lead a new initiative. When the time is right and you're a bit
better known, try making a move to bring yourself more into
the center of things. If you're on a forum, offer to moderate.
If you have specialized knowledge, offer to help people or
host a get-together. Becoming a doer helps you become a
player in your space.
5. Profit! Okay, we're kidding. But seriously, small, daily action
helps. And being inside the right community is a great way to
build business, glean insider knowledge, and get an edge in
your niche. Follow these five steps and you'll be on your way.

Businesses That Understand How "One of Us" Works

There is no vast and inclusive list of every company that has the
trust agent thing figured out, but because we have attend conferences and know people virtually who espouse the very lessons
we're hoping to share with you, we wanted to direct your attention
to a few shining examples of the people we think of as One of Us.

Frank Eliason: Comcast Cares

Who knew that searching for this company's name on Twitter
would lead to a full-time job with a staff of seven and more
massive mainstream press than any customer service initiative
has probably ever received (i.e., if you count only positive
experiences). From its humble beginnings as an unsanctioned
experiment to a full-fledged group with processes within the

company, Comcast has understood who they need to be. Many other companies want to hear what Eliason did, and why.

Eliason says:

> Like most companies, Comcast has been listening in to the blogosphere for quite some time. In the fall of 2007 we started to get more involved in the conversation by reaching out to our customers to help. This led to further discussion and a positive buzz. As this buzz grew, we developed it into a team of trust agents to act as Customer Ambassadors throughout the Internet. It was now February 2007. We started to share customer stories with leadership throughout the company. This led a VP, Scott Westerman, to guide us to check out a place called Twitter. When we first did our search, it was enough to make our heads spin. Like all spaces, we listened for some time before interacting. It is important, if you want to be successful in these spaces, to know the audience and what level of interaction is acceptable. We watched for two months, learned a lot about how people viewed Comcast and how we could help. It still amazes me that a simple message "Can I help?" sent as a response to a tweet could generate such buzz in the blogosphere and mainstream press. Customer Service can be hip!
>
> The key is not just listening but utilizing the information to continually improve. Nothing is more powerful than sharing data but then tying it to the customer story in their words. Web 2.0 is perfect for that! It is slightly more powerful when you tie the data to Grannie Annie, than just a number. Working on sharing the story for many organizations, I have found this space to be an extremely powerful method because it is the customers own words and easy to obtain. Simple tools such as Google Blogsearch or Twitter Search and you can put together the story.

Now we listen and participate in many Web 2.0 spaces on the Internet, but Twitter is the one that has become the most known. The reason I find it so beneficial is individuals are answering a simple question: "What are you doing?" So if people are talking about your brand, they will be discussing it among the many users of Twitter. It is truly the here and now. Our success in this space, in my opinion, is based on the personal approach and just the goal of helping. We do not work from a sales or PR perspective, but rather a way to help. It is that easy.

When we see Eliason at a conference, we think of him as the tireless face of Comcast's alternative customer service efforts. Sure, he's not solving phone call hold times (except for the clever small percentage of people who have learned that they can get faster service via Twitter). Sure, he's not improving the core products or rolling out the future of cable. Eliason's not even getting into the fights that roll around the Internet with regard to Net neutrality (the controversy about whether the Internet should be metered, traffic-shaped, and otherwise). It's not his job.

Eliason's job is embracing customers and being helpful, and he does it exceptionally well. Now that he's training a team to operate the same way, completely through the loosely joined online perspective, his rise as a trust agent continues to soar even higher and faster.

But the *most* important point as it relates to the whole lesson about One of Us is this: Eliason doesn't have to evangelize about himself, his company, or anything related to what he's doing for us or for the online media world. *We* do it for him. He's built hundreds of microevangelists out of us, just because we love how he approached this and because he used Twitter in a way that we all felt it could be used, but that other companies hadn't yet embraced.

Lionel Menchaca: Dell.com

The story is so overused in tech circles that it's probably frayed and tattered, but in case you missed it, here's the short version: Jeff Jarvis, superfamous blogger, has a problem with his Dell laptop. Turns out there are others who have a similar problem. Jeff blogs about it. *Many* people blog about it. Suddenly, Google's search results for Dell all say "Dell Hell" and go to stories of laptop issues.

Enter Lionel Menchaca, Michael Dell's blogger of record, who's been really interested in blogging and is thrilled to be thrown in the game. With lots of effort and nuance, Menchaca got involved, became One of Us, turned the sentiment of the wronged Dell users on its head, and helped communicate about resources during the corrective actions that fix most people's problems.

Flash forward to 2008 and Menchaca frequently attends conferences and speaks on panels and solo about how companies can use blogging and other social media to reach out and build stronger relationships. He is at the center of initiatives such as using Twitter (@LionelAtDELL) and taking advantage of listening technology.

And Menchaca's not alone. The modern trust agent organization has several people focused on doing similarly great work. Richard Binhammer is another personality within Dell who has become One of Us. The bench over there runs deep. Dozens of Dell employees are out there on Twitter and Facebook, connecting, being helpful, and being part of the larger community.

Daniela Barbosa: Synaptica (a Dow Jones Company)

Stop us if you've heard this one before: A young woman (let's make her an immigrant who moved to the United States when she was nine) drives cross country from her job on Wall Street with Dow Jones Factiva, the monstrous media property that reports on the state of the financial world every day and provides access to over 10,000 aggregate premium feeds. She sneaks off into the world of Web 2.0 and free content to face all the cool tech companies and their challenges. Shortly thereafter, Barbosa proceeds to turn the company inside out with regard to blogging, to taxonomy and folksonomy, to well-produced e-books with custom design in place of your typical stodgy white papers.

When she's not attending conferences like Defrag, the Web 2.0 Expo, and other places where the rest of us spend time, Barbosa works with the Data Portability project. She also serves as the internal go-to person for blogging, both internally (within the enterprise) and externally.

We asked Twitter who might be another great example of a trust agent to include in the book, and a good half-dozen people mentioned Barbosa. They knew her by reputation, by her blog, and by what she represented to us: One of Us inside Dow Jones. Barbosa had this to say:

> The thing that I however am the most proud of is not the traffic or the response but the fact that my Dow Jones colleagues are starting to get into it (and I hope it isn't just because I ask them to!). Recently, the Dow Jones Taxonomy Team was at the Enterprise Search and Taxonomy Bootcamp, and most of the team blogged about what they learned from there.

Because Barbosa can bring that sense of being One of Us to the various groups she participates in, and because she shares so much back and forth between B2B enterprises and the larger tech and social communities, she certainly makes the grade as a trust agent who exemplifies the concept of being One of Us.

Trust Agents Are Not Infiltrators

Before this book came out, we wrote an e-book titled *Trust Economies*, and, before that, Julien had published one of his own, *Keep It Real*, on the subject of marketers who were trying to speak to communities they weren't a part of. We've heard arguments suggesting marketing types understanding the people they're speaking to is like saying they should be spies, betraying their community for profit at the drop of a hat. We strongly disagree with that premise.

The way we've always envisioned trust agents is that they are not phony. They don't join a community they don't care about, both because it wouldn't be in their business interests to do so and because they want to sleep at night. To us, there is no worse crime than being fake, and it's never something we suggest anyone else do.

Trust agents aren't infiltrators. Communities (or anyone, really) can sniff out pretense and blacklist those individuals immediately. And, with the giant reputation system that is the Web, it is not advantageous to be known for trying to fake your way into someone's tribe. They can tell, and they'll tell everyone.

A Final Lesson: Don't Be "That Guy"

"That Guy" can be a man or a woman, but we all know a version of That Guy. He's annoying. He handed you his business card immediately but barely looks at yours. His attitude is "hand them all out," which is the business equivalent of carpet bombing. He talks about his company all the time, but you can tell his smile isn't very genuine while he's doing it—maybe it's even a bit desperate. He isn't the best person to spend time with, and eventually, you'll be avoiding his calls.

There's a saying, "If you look around a poker table and can't spot a sucker, it's you." Well, it's the same with being That Guy. Don't let it happen to you.

You may love your company, and that's great; we would all love to be in that position. And you may want it to succeed so badly that you dream about it. If so, awesome. But it takes a special mix of ego, humility, empathy, and sales acumen to be able to be That Guy without being loathed, and most people don't have it. We definitely don't. Very few do, and if you're not 100 percent sure that you can pull it off, you shouldn't even try, because it'll be a train wreck. Worse, it might be a train wreck that no one will even tell you about; you'll just slowly see responses to your e-mails taking longer and longer, you'll be making fewer sales, and so on, and you won't know why. But it'll be because you're That Guy.

In your business, you shouldn't ask for anything almost ever. Asking for favors, getting people to blog things for you, these are things that make people go out of their way and that make them feel uncomfortable.

A trust agent's job is the opposite: to make people feel comfortable, all the way, building deep relationships before ever asking something of others. You should be there for *them*.

Another part of this is humility. You may love your brand, but don't just assume everyone does or that they want to hear about it all the time. The way we see it, a brand representative doesn't need to verbalize, and shouldn't even need to verbalize, their love; they should live it. A Starbucks trust agent should be all about warmth and relaxation, because that's what Starbucks is about; he or she doesn't have to be talking about coffee all the time.

We're both careful about this. We love our projects, but we really try to be careful about looking like shills, both because it's disgusting to us and because it shortchanges our reputation. We're always looking at the long term, which is completely unlike That Guy, because he tries to sell to *everyone*, which explains the business card thing.

The thing is, *everyone* is not your customer, and *everyone* isn't the audience you want to influence, which is the difference between a trust agent and a "brand evangelist." Trust agents don't just evangelize; in fact, they plant seeds so that there can instead be a kind of mass evangelism (as mentioned earlier), whereby word (the message!) spreads on its own.

If you take one lesson away from this chapter, take this: Don't be That Guy. We don't mind companies in our space, and we need good people working with us, but we can't stand another one of those people trying to sell us stuff. We're sick of it, and so is everyone else.

4

Archimedes Effect

BETH KANTER IS a force to be reckoned with in the technology not-for-profit space. She is a passionate, energetic woman who seems to be forever in motion. One night, at a Boston-based tech gathering, Kanter mentioned her latest project to Chris: "I'm working on sending a Cambodian woman to college. Today, I raised $500 toward my goal of $1,000, and I was wondering if you could help me get the other half tomorrow." Chris said yes. It's not easy to say no to Kanter. She supports the best causes.

Chris decided to ask the community on Twitter to support the cause. He tweeted a message that read, "Spend $10 and send a woman to college," with a link to Beth's blog post, which had a simple widget that would let one send money. Subsequent messages on Twitter said, "For the price of two lattes, you can send a woman to college today." Chris asked that his followers on Twitter "re-tweet," to help spread the message, along with the link. This request turned the message viral, as other people on Twitter with different followers sent the request out into their communities.

Using these simple techniques, the additional $500 was raised on Twitter in less than two hours.

Kanter explains, "My first campaign took three weeks of blogging, e-mailing, and IM'ing people I had a connection with. After that I did two other campaigns, and because I built relationships with the donors of the first campaign, they donated again and asked their friends as well." If you construct your request to illustrate a compelling outcome, have a specific call to action (e.g., "Give me ten bucks"), and build your community organically, then you will probably be successful.

Chris has several thousand followers on Twitter, so the results will be different depending on your reach. But the premise and the method still hold true: Online communities are valuable. They can be reached more quickly and leveraged more effectively, and the right kind of trust agent can work with those communities to effect actionable change. Understanding of how online communities work can help you leverage them for good causes or for business value. The tools available now are better than ever.

The Archimedes Effect

Why do we use power tools when a good saw and hammer will do the job? Why do we ride bicycles instead of walk? If we're happy with the way things are, why do we seek something new? For most of us, the reason we use new tools is because they will get results faster or more effectively. We seek to do the same in all our activities.

Do you want more customers? Do you want to take what you have and turn it into something more? Do you want to know how best to use your Internet presence for good? That's where we get closer to what this chapter is about.

Technology is taken for granted every day. Instruments such as the bicycle are so common that they are barely seen as technology at all. In reality, we use bicycles or cars to get around because they're faster, and we use power tools because they will help us build a stronger house. Yet when people connect with the Web to do their business, they often ignore tools that, again and again, have helped others get ahead. Trust agents understand this and strive to learn how the Web can make things happen: more, faster, bigger, whatever needle needs moving.

Archimedes of Syracuse was a famous inventor from the third century BC. He's the one who said "Eureka." He also said, "With a lever large enough, I can move the world." The Archimedes Effect is about leverage: putting in a certain amount of effort and getting a greater result than our normal human effort would give. Everyone uses leverage every day: Business owners hire employees so that their business can do more; people use technology such as cars to help them get to work faster; companies have systems that allow them to be more efficient. Yet millions use the Web every day and ignore how best to use the tools at their disposal to bring the greatest benefit.

There's a programmer's saying that "the lazy ones are usually the best." It may seem counterintuitive, but it's true. Programmers want a little bit of code to do a lot of work, so the lazy programmers usually do the most thinking and the least writing. They maximize their time by having the code they write do all the heavy lifting, and the best ones do it even more effectively than the rest, picking up code here and there, then combining it with very powerful results. Result: Lots of power, a lot less work.

A Basic View of Leverage

The simplest way to understand leveraging the Web is this: You can use the advantage you have in one place to help you in another. Like the programmers, you can use what you have a lot of (in their case, brains) to achieve more, and you can do it more easily.

Apple used its market dominance with the iPod as a springboard to the creation of the iPhone. Can you remember another phone device launch that had so much press coverage? Can you remember mile-long lines and sellouts for any other phone in the history of mobile devices? Leverage means taking what works and moving the value into something else that's different (yet connected) to the previous idea.

Kevin Rose leveraged his success with the popular social news site Digg.com into the opportunity to make an online video platform, Revision3. He used the leverage he gained from those two successes to make a messaging platform, Pownce. He was no match for the Twitter, the competition he was after, but it went a lot better than it would have if he had started from nothing. Because he and his team had his previous successes and the reputation associated with them, the platform had a bit of an opportunity to develop. Viewing all three products in sum—a social news site, a video media platform, and a communications platform—you might be able to see future opportunities that Rose could leverage as well.

Celebrities use leverage all the time. Robert Downey Jr. staged one of the biggest comebacks in entertainment history with his role as Tony Stark in the 2008 hit, *Iron Man*, which took in $98 million dollars on its opening weekend and exceeded half a billion dollars in ticket sales in a few months. He went right from that film to the reasonably successful *Tropic Thunder*, then to *The Soloist*, and on to Guy Ritchie's *Sherlock Holmes*. The star's success in one film can be leveraged to land another, which shows his consistent star power, which in turn allows him even further leverage. He withdraws some equity from the roles he's successfully completed and utilizes it in future products.

Donald Trump lives in the world of leveraging opportunities. Real estate investing at Trump's level is all about leverage: He pulls money out of previous successes and uses it to invest in new projects. Trump does the same with his fame, too. He leveraged his wealth into the entertainment field with the TV show *The Apprentice*, with Mark Burnett, and then leveraged his new visibility as a mentor on the show to launch a series of online courses called Trump University.

Understanding leverage, and how to think about it, is one of the trickier parts of being a trust agent. This might be the least native part of what some of you know how to do. And yet, for others, this is a huge "well duh!" chapter. Chris, for instance, is less skilled in applying leverage than Julien. He compensates with other trust agent skills, but certainly looks for ways to improve his understanding and application of leverage.

An Introduction to Arbitrage

Another example of leverage is arbitrage, something used across the Web most famously by pay-per-click (PPC) specialists in the early days of search advertising. It works like this: You buy something somewhere at one price, then sell it somewhere else at a higher price. PPC marketers did this with clicks, buying traffic at one price and selling it at another.

To explain this further, imagine that a company comes to you and says, "I have to get more people to buy my rain gutter replacement system." You can sell it the old-fashioned way, by taking out advertisements, by dialing numbers from the phone book, by posting a web site with a big fat "Buy now" button—or you can take advantage of search engine marketing.

Build a web site with all kinds of useful information on rain gutter replacement systems. Have plenty of links for people to click to purchase such a system. Does that magically make people come there when they want a rain gutter replacement system? No.

The solution is to buy search traffic from Google, which sells certain search terms for certain dollar amounts, such that when people are searching Google (or any site where Google AdSense ads are placed) and click a link, you (the person who bought the search traffic and paid money for the ads) pay a certain amount. For example, if you make $30 every time you sign up a customer seeking rain gutter replacement, and it costs you $10 worth of search traffic advertising to get those links, you make $20 for every successful procedure. Voilà: You have arbitrage as a lever-age system as it pertains to basic Web commerce.

A Young Man's Primer

When Julien was young, he had what he thought was a brilliant idea (young people often think they're smarter than they really are). The way he saw it, the most powerful currency in the world was the British pound, so he would move to England, work there, gather a bit of savings, and then move to India and live like a prince. It seemed to make a lot of sense; save one kind of currency that's common to the British, then trade it somewhere else where it's worth a lot. Turns out, this is kind of what currency traders do, and it's kind of what George Soros famously did when he broke the Bank of England by shorting the pound in 1992, for an eventual profit of $2 billion. (We now realize they're in the wrong line of work.)

The principle of arbitrage is the same everywhere, and while it's used widely for trade and currency, the concept can be applied elsewhere as well. Arbitrage is using something that is less valuable to one person and benefiting from its greater value to someone else. When Julien's show was on Sirius satellite radio, it wasn't that big a deal to him, but it had the effect that most people in traditional media *did* take him *a lot* more seriously. As a consequence, he was using something that, to him, was not particularly valuable to help him gain entrance to some places where he really did want to be.

To understand leverage, it helps to hear about what Jane McGonigal, award-winning game designer, calls *multicapitalism*, or the ability to understand multiple, varying forms of value and to know how to exchange one type of capital freely for another. Advantages are gained from having various economies (trading stocks, or favors, being an easy example we're all familiar with) because many people do not understand them very clearly. The reason an exporter from Morocco is able to make money in the United States is because very few people go to Morocco or know how to speak the language, and because the exporter isn't competing with, say, Mickey Mouse dolls, which anyone has access to and can sell.

The issue of reduced competition is extremely beneficial when it comes to leverage: Under such circumstances, profits can increase massively. Julian Dibbell, *Wired* contributor and game enthusiast, was able to take advantage of this kind of leverage in the game world, trading virtual, online goods in a massive-multiplayer online (MMO) game known as Ultima Online, eventually becoming the second most successful trader in the game, resulting in thousands of dollars of profit. He was able to do this because almost no one knew how to make a living this way, which reduced competition and made the job easier.

Whether you're leveraging a virtual, in-game economy (see the following sidebars) or leveraging attention on your blog to help with another project, the point is the same. Leveraging technology, information, or anything else will increase the value of what you do many times over.

In-Game Economies and Leverage (by Chris Penn)

Think that leverage, arbitrage, and information scarcity are the domain of business only? Think again. World of Warcraft, the popular online role-playing game, has an entire economy built into it with free markets that players can use to buy, sell, and trade goods. In virtual locations like the Auction House, tens of thousands of goods change hands daily for in-game currency.

Those players who want to do more than just swap items can install additional pieces of software that give them every tool they need to dominate the markets in the game, such as Auctioneer, which keeps detailed records of average buy and sell prices, item scarcity, and much more. This is information arbitrage at its highest level—knowing far more about the markets in the game than the average player, you know immediately which items are for sale at deeply undervalued prices, can buy them out, and resell them immediately for significant profits. Where the average player earns a few dozen gold a day playing the game, the best arbitrageurs earn thousands of gold a day with comparatively little effort.

Where this truly shines is not in the game itself, but in what it teaches and how it trains the minds of those who play the gold making part of the game. The ideas of leverage, arbitrage, and information disparity are not new to business, but it opens the eyes of people who would otherwise never be exposed to the concepts. In turn, these players develop practical, hands-on experience at arbitrage and learn that when it comes to making huge amounts of capital, real or virtual, the power lies not in production or manufacturing, but in arbitrage.

The Path of Least Resistance

While we're on the subject of reduced competition, using the Web to network and make connections may be the easiest thing you've ever done. This means connecting on a personal level rather than a business one, so neither party wants anything from the other. (See Chapter 3, "One of Us" for more about this.) In a way, the Web is the equivalent of chatting in a bar, though it's the largest bar in the world, where superficial connection with almost anyone is possible. In that environment, we get to have an initial relationship, but it can be used as a foundation to build on later. The easiest way to build on that relationship is in person.

Meeting someone in person with whom you've already connected on the Web is more effective, because you get all the signals of a real relationship, including nonverbal cues (facial expression, tone of voice, etc.). And after connecting on the Web, meeting people in person can be like meeting an old friend; you get to catch up on all the stuff you don't know about them.

Whatever your industry, it is important to meet a lot of people online, if only superficially. You can do this by connecting with them through tools like Facebook and Twitter or by commenting on their sites. Then find ways to meet face-to-face—whether at industry conferences or in one-on-one meetings—to cement those relationships. By doing so, you make yourself more "real" than the competition (i.e., the people that aren't there in person) and give yourself an advantage. It's easier to own the game.

Owning the Largest Game in the World

Google brought a whole new level of search accuracy to the Internet when Larry Page and Sergey Brin created a system based on the powerful algorithm, PageRank. This system indexed the Web with a far more effective form of measuring web site relevance than before. Ten years later, the first thing that comes to mind when one thinks of Google is "search." The company's name has even slipped into everyday use as a verb: "Could you Google the store's address for me?" Of course, the Google of 10 years ago wasn't the $125 billion market cap company it is now; in fact, it barely had a business model.

But if you think Google is a search company, you're missing one of the biggest and best examples of leveraging technology. Google took its advanced ability to know what people wanted to find and paired that with advertising, building the best contextual advertising placement that the Web had ever seen. Now, billions of dollars are pouring into Google for a platform that it has paired with several of its other offerings, adding more and more value to the company's leverage effort.

Tools like Google give us another example of what leveraging resources can do for us. Take one opportunity, grow it into something of quality, and then leverage that opportunity into a new one that derives even more value. See where this could be useful for you as a trust agent? Leverage is part of what drives the more successful people on the Web.

Want another example? Kevin Ham, a devout Christian from Vancouver, tagged as "the man who owns the Internet" by *Business 2.0* magazine, owns hundreds of thousands of domain names, including God.com and Satan.com. But it was his agreement with the government of Cameroon that marked him as the domain owner to watch. By recognizing that many people mistyped domain names into the address bar, he was able to make one of the greatest deals in the history of the Web. You see, every time you mistype .com as .cm, you are asking for a Web address in Cameroon. Ham made a big deal with the government there, so now, whenever someone mistypes a .com address as .cm, and it's unregistered (e.g., Live.cm, Microsoft's search engine, is registered and points to Live.com, but chrisbrogan.cm isn't), it redirects that person to one of Ham's web sites. This one massive move created millions of additional views to Ham's sites, and as with Google, it's all a matter of leveraging infrastructures that are already in place.

Existing Infrastructure

No one tries to build a well behind their house anymore because we all have running water in our homes. We take public transit because it makes our commutes easier, helping us get to our jobs so we can earn money, so we can pay our rent, so we can keep the wheels of society moving around and around. Infrastructure exists everywhere in the modern world because it's a time saver, letting us focus on the things we're best at for as long as possible. When we're using our time to best advantage, we're better serving ourselves and our families and communities. As a result, everyone benefits.

Somehow, the connection made with infrastructure in our everyday world is still lost on most people who use the Web. While we do see both e-mail and Google as utilities, for the most part, we don't see the infrastructure that's present there, and thus we don't see how it can grease the wheels of our vehicle, helping us get where we want to go. Some people *do* see it, and they're the ones who are quickest to get rich, whether in either social capital, financial capital, or (sometimes) both. Those who leverage work that other people have done (after all, Google was built by people) are able to profit mostly because they're not busy re-inventing the wheel. For the most part, these people are business owners. To start seeing like one is to see opportunity everywhere, just waiting for you to show up and take it.

How a Trust Agent Uses Time

Once you learn how to better leverage time, you free yourself up to do the work that's most important. If we haven't made it abundantly clear, this isn't the *easy* route to success. (We know there's no easy route, right?) With trust agents, finding the time to apply the human touch to thousands of people in your network (provided you've done your Agent Zero work well) is important. To do this you must learn how to leverage your time.

Some of the simpler ways require a great deal of discipline and sometimes some negotiation. For instance, how long is your commute to the office? Is that time something that could be leveraged more effectively elsewhere? Are you willing to make that proposal to your boss? As we said before, Chris's commute in 2008 was 67 miles one way, which (with traffic) amounted to almost four hours in the car every day. Shifting that one variable into more keyboard time meant that both Chris and his company were happier with the results.

Can you find ways to save time and then leverage that savings elsewhere? Absolutely. There are plenty of ways.

Leveraging Relationships

In a way, personal networking is a bit like leveraging relationships. The problem with saying this is that it sounds like that old-fashioned version of networking instead of the One of Us or Agent Zero methods that prove more effective and easier to establish. While many worry about how people perceive those who leverage business relationships, there are also many positive aspects.

Does this apply in the business sense? Absolutely. We tend to do business with people who are like us. Beyond that, it's more likely that we do business with people we feel emotionally positive about. If you had the opportunity to offer business to two qualified people, and all things were equal except that one of those people had helped you close business with a big supplier, which one might you lean toward? Regardless of what's fair or what systems are in place, there's a positive bias toward the person who helped you.

When you switch jobs, is it easier to cold-call some company or to reach out to a friend at that company who can vouch for you? In the latter case, you've leveraged a relationship with a friend with the hope the friend might be willing to help you by vouching for you and by facilitating introductions to the people who can help you get the job.

If you build a circle of friends at an event, one benefit is that people who might benefit from meeting each other for business reasons connect. For instance, if we help connect Beth Kanter with a paid speaking opportunity, we've expended some amount of our leverage and translated it into goodwill with Kanter. And, as we've discussed before with regard to social capital, this act actually benefits all parties. The people seeking the speaker get a great talent. Kanter gets a paid opportunity, plus the potential for future business. And we get an emotional resonance with Kanter as the people who put it together, which might benefit us should we need to leverage some of Kanter's resources later on.

You can see how tricky it is to write about this without running the risk of sounding like leveraging your relationships is the equivalent of using people. This must not be the case if you are to establish successful relationships. Doing favors so that people owe you favors must *not* be the motivation behind developing these relationships. Do favors because you like someone, because it's the right thing to do, or because you like to be helpful. The result is that you accrue social capital *as a side benefit* of doing good, but doing good by itself is its own reward.

Is it wrong to think that what you do for someone will be (eventually) reciprocated? No. Is it wrong to *expect* it? You betcha. Don't operate with favor trading in mind. That shifts the relationship dynamic strongly toward people feeling that you're always tallying, that you're looking for something whenever you come calling, along with several other personality traits that don't bode well for long-term relationships. Instead, just create goodwill. You'll see better results and sleep better at night. We promise.

Standing Out by Standing Tall

One way to build up a reputation that you can leverage is by being one of the boldest or best in what you do. This relates closely to Chapter 2, "Make Your Own Game." A guy like Gary Vaynerchuk of WineLibrary.com isn't famous because he made a Web show about wine. He's not famous because he learned a new way to sell wine to the world. Vaynerchuk is famous because he sweats passion and bleeds enthusiasm. Vaynerchuk is driven the way the robot from *The Terminator* is driven (if the robot could shout). There could be a hundred Internet video shows about wine, but Vaynerchuk made late-night TV host Conan O'Brien eat dirt and a cigar, and that makes Vaynerchuk a god.

What this has to do with leveraging relationships is everything: Vaynerchuk signed a big book deal because he was *the* wine guy on the Internet. He has a Hollywood agent because he was the most passionate guy doing useful content that the mainstream wanted as much as the "nerderati" did. Vaynerchuk then took all that leveraging power and launched his Gourmet Library product: He had all that goodwill, money, and Internet power and knew he could point it at a new product.

ACTION: First Steps to Leverage Your Position within an Organization

You want to rock your corporation the way Vaynerchuk rocked wine? You've gotta stand tall. Some first moves in this space:

- *Be bold about your business purpose*—Vaynerchuk isn't active and passionate without having an end goal in mind. He made over $55 million more in his wine business through exposure on his video show and Web presence.
- *Be everywhere*—Vaynerchuk puts out a consistent show, a personal blog, lots of videos, and that's just on the Web. He hit the conference circuit hard in 2008, and 2009 was even bigger.
- *Be a salesperson*—Vaynerchuk asks for the sale all the time. If he's building his database, he asks for more names. If he's pushing book sales, he asks you to buy three copies each.
- *Be relentless*—Vaynerchuk is just a human being, but that's hard to believe. He gets up early. He goes to bed late. He works every angle he can manage. Every day. All the time.
- *Be gracious*—Vaynerchuk loves his fans. He loves his supporters. He is passionate about the people who raise him up, and he promotes them. Anyone who wants to grow their business or their platform can learn from Gary.

If you're thinking somewhere in your head that you need permission to learn how to start building the ability to leverage the resources for your corporation, hand this book to someone else. You've already lost the game.

Protecting Your Community as a Leverage Point

Here is a rule of thumb that works really well when it comes to leveraging your relationship with your audience: Don't ever sell to your audience. Instead, be their gatekeeper.

Think of Oprah Winfrey. She gives and gives, constantly, and leverages that goodwill into bigger and bigger guests and giveaways. But does she ever try to sell her audience directly? No, Winfrey leverages her audience to provide visibility: to stars, to movies, to car companies. She protects her audience by guarding them from the bad stuff, and she lets the good stuff pass through, making her audience even happier as a result. (See Figure 4.1.)

Building any kind of following online is difficult enough. It requires solid leadership skills, the ability to create a sense of belonging, a gracious attitude, transparency about who you are, and empowering the community to feel important. It gets a

Figure 4.1 Preserve Trust by Protecting Your Networks and Communications

lot harder when, to participate in a community, members are asked for money to sustain your business. In fact, it is practically impossible to foster a sense of community under these circumstances unless your channel is already very financially motivated (the "make money online" bloggers come to mind).

Celebrities use the Oprah Winfrey method regularly on Oscar night, using their visibility to obtain the most expensive and beautiful designer dresses in the world. They don't pay for them. The designers know that their names will be all over tabloids and television the next day, so they give Oscar attendees their best stuff for free, and celebrities leverage the attention to benefit.

Jeff Pulver, one of the pioneers of the VoIP industry, also did this well when he ran the VON conferences. He charged a great deal of money for people to attend the event, because corporations would pay for their employees to attend, knowing that those attendees would learn from true visionaries and future thinkers and that this information would invigorate their disrupted industry. The employees themselves never paid to attend. Pulver would then turn around and spend a good portion of the money he collected to provide the attendees a memorable time, including flying in rock bands like the Counting Crows to play at open-bar events, where Pulver did his best to dance with all 2,000 attendees.

Pulver would then charge exhibitors tens of thousands of dollars so they could gain access to his beloved community. They paid because Pulver attracted the brightest minds in communications technologies to the events. The exhibitors considered this part of their marketing budget. The corporations paid for the attendees. Pulver paid for the fun. The people who didn't have to pay at all? The heart and soul of the community. This ecosystem lasted for over a decade and served everyone's business needs rather well.

Daniel Palestrant runs what is probably the most profitable online professional network you've never heard about. Sermo .com is a network for medical professionals. It's exclusive. You need to demonstrate your credentials to become a member, but once you're inside, you gain business relationships with the brightest minds in medicine and surgical arts.

Palestrant charges media and investment types a fee to access his community, ask questions, or seek professional endorsement opportunities. The community at large opts in for this kind of matchmaking, and they get financial benefits from their interactions with the paid professionals. Here again, there's a professional ecosystem that treats the audience or community as the most important asset and requires a fee from those parties who want access to it.

This is a winning formula for certain types of trust agents. Are you one of them? Make sure that you are, because this kind of strategy can be a lot of work.

Note: This little section doesn't pertain directly to how companies make money. In that particular case, the best approach is to sell products and services that empower and equip people to do something for themselves such that they are grateful they gave you money in exchange for those resources. Apple does this particularly well. We shell out a few hundred dollars to possess a phone that is every bit as much a status symbol as it is a communications platform. We buy the thinnest laptop in the world and pay a premium for fewer features. We do this because we perceive that the devices and software and design will equip us to do more with our lives.

But we believe there's a lesson here for that type of company, too.

Tools We Use for Time Leverage

Looking for some quick, practical ways to leverage your time more efficiently? Here are just a few tools of the trade for a time-starved trust agent:

- **Spinvox.com:** Why listen to voice mail when you can have it transposed and sent to you as text? You can read faster than you can listen.
- **Jott.com:** Speak into your phone and you can receive an e-mail of your transcribed words. Easy leverage.
- **Kayak.com:** Check several airlines and hotels at the same time for prices from a single screen.
- **SMS:** Use this for e-mail. It makes the message and response more concise. It cuts down e-mail clutter.
- **Podcasts:** As learning tools, we can consume these during travel/transit.
- **RSS reader:** Instead of going to blogs directly, we read them quickly via an RSS reader.
- **Keyboard shortcuts:** For most every application we use, we learn the keyboard shortcuts. This time does add up.

How a Trust Agent Leverages Social Media

Social media like blogging, podcasting, video, and using social networks like Facebook, Twitter. The newer platforms provide opportunities for trust agents to leverage communication mediums to the benefit of their organizations. First and foremost, reaching out to people via blogging is a one-to-many opportunity. Instead of sending a single e-mail or placing a phone call, having someone like Lionel Menchaca from Dell writing about service issues on the Direct2Dell blog is a way to stretch the value of that message so that it resonates with more people.

Being Frank Eliason and using Twitter to respond to people as @comcastcares means leveraging the medium to achieve many positive outcomes: It lowers repeat calls to customer service; it reduces escalation issues within the care department; it also provides outward signs that the company is doing something with the customer's complaint.

The reason Eliason is able to achieve all this is because he leverages massive social networks that let him know when people are talking about his company. Without real-time assessments of what conversations are happening, and where, do you think it would be possible to reach them fast enough to put out the fires? With all of the resources available today, not using them is a lot like being a fire station with no phone. Shouldn't you be using that phone?

Doing more with what is available to you in this case means sending out responses and having steady community interaction by using the open-faced interactions of the Web to build two-way relationships and conversations instead of using the old, one-at-a-time methods from other means of communication. You can see how this might apply to your business, too.

Fish Where the Fish Are

Another point to consider: If you're not taking advantage of the way the Web connects everyone, including your potential customers, you're missing the easy opportunities. Have you checked out Woot.com? Matt Rutledge built a site where people rush to buy a single discount item a day and where hundreds more level their reviews, commentary, and more for every product put up there. The reviews are often harsh, yet sellers are seeing the benefits. *Inc.* magazine reported in a September 2008 article that

Rutledge has reported a three-year growth of 4,998 percent. How? By taking advantage of the technology of the Web that allows for two-way conversations, for peer review, and for an entertainment-like experience built into the shopping.

Dell has created an entire ad campaign by promoting its sales and discounts via Twitter (www.dell.com/twitter). It provides sales for zero dollars of effort, meaning that the ROI on leveraging this medium is pretty darned good.

The Web has made building relationships an inexpensive-to-free proposition, and that part is good. The reason for trust agents, however, is that this is an opt-in world, and your buyer has more control of your attempts to sell than ever before. Tuning out is just as easy and free as your attempts to bring a message across these new channels.

That said, there are benefits to using the Web as a tool to reach more people.

About Recommendation

One of the reasons the Web's citizens tend to provide free stuff for people is that they are leveraging the huge potential audience for any product or service, along with their idea's ability to be widely spread at little to no cost. Whether it's free blog content, a "freemium" service that asks you to pay if you want more features, or anything in between, the Web's ability to reach thousands of people is pretty much unparalleled, if you know how.

Leveraging the social Web's ability to widely disseminate ideas through recommendation engines like Digg, StumbleUpon, and others helps you communicate your ideas to hundreds of people without using a megaphone. Instead, you can quietly say what you have to say and let your audience spread your message for you. This allows you to focus on creating more content, creating more deals, and forging more partnerships. In fact, the more you can get other people to relay your ideas, the better it ends up being. This recommendation is a great tool to employ.

The difficulty in creating content that will get a recommendation, the one that most companies tend to get wrong, is that they don't think creatively about how their content can be exciting to the average population. This is a common problem; if you've been in your industry for a while, it's probably pretty boring to you unless you just developed something revolutionary.

The trick is to come up with something you could tell people at a party, to be able to differentiate between what *you* think is interesting about what you do and what the average person thinks is interesting.

Things to Stop and Things to Start

If you're busy trying to reinvent the wheel because it makes you happy and you enjoy solving problems, that's fine. But if you're like most of us and just want to get to the good stuff, work to make a better product, or whatever, here's some commonsense advice about where to spend your time.

Stop Trying to Find Readers for Your Blog

Some people spend all their time trying to tell one person at a time about their newest Web site, hoping it will take off. How well do you think that works? Imagine standing on the street corner with a stack of your leaflets, trying to hand them out to busy people as they walk by. Sometimes asking for more readers, or pestering people in social news sites, or e-mailing your latest post is the online equivalent. Whatever your strategy, you must ask yourself, is it working? If you answer yes, how much work is that taking? How many hours? Is this really the best use of your time?

Start Enabling Your Existing Readers to Talk about You

Make sure people can subscribe to your blog via RSS, that they can have it sent to their e-mail box. Add plug-ins to your blog that let people recommend your stuff to the most popular social news sites. Give people posts that inspire their own thinking and that promote sharing. Offer resources that people will want to share naturally and that will move your information along nicely without you having to babysit it all. Don't worry about driving attention. Instead, make your material more accessible and more shareable, then move on.

Stop Doing Your Own Books and Research

Finding opportunities to leverage resources means understanding what tasks need doing by *you* versus need doing. Are you analyzing every single aspect of your business? Are you trying out every tool and joining every social network? Are you reading every blog post and buying every new book on the Internet?

Start Looking for a Personal Research Assistant and Aggregators

Learning how to use an assistant can be complicated. There are a variety of ways in which you can have others help out with certain tasks that need doing so that you have time to work on the more complex tasks. By getting this help, you are providing work for others and freeing up your time to do even more.

Stop Spending Money and Time Building Your Web Site

The first Internet required that you spend $30,000 (or more!) on a web site that would be your calling card to the world. You'd be ready for business if you had a site that showed off your products and where people could order them. After years of trying to convince people that they needed such things, companies finally started listening. Web design shops began to flourish. Today there are thousands of talented companies looking to build robust, custom web sites for you that are loaded with features promising to help you do business at an affordable price.

Start Looking at Prefab Solutions Like WordPress and Drupal

In recent years, things have changed. There are free software solutions that work just great as web sites, and they come loaded with reasons why they're the best fit for a platform. Both WordPress and Drupal cost no money to install, and both have active communities of developers and designers making even more software available. But the key is leveraging. Why make a production out of creating a site and a design and functionality when there are simpler ways to leverage existing technology and move forward?

Stop Telling Everyone about Your New Thing

Not everyone needs to know about your project! In fact, the more they hear about it from other people instead of from you, the more convinced they will be by this social proofing. Telling one person at a time won't make a difference. Your project must be sticky and spreadable, all at once.

Start Crowdsourcing

Crowdsourcing is the ability to have access to many people at a time and to have them perform one small task each, like the earlier example of Chris raising money through Twitter. Using mass-collaboration tools allows you to bypass the short attention span of a large amount of people, helping you achieve large goals quickly. This is how Ron Paul actually gave himself a chance in the Republican primaries of 2008, even though he wants to dismantle the Federal Reserve. If he can do it, so can you. Find your audience and leverage their power (more on this later).

Summing Up the Stops and Starts

Whatever industry you're in, leverage your position in your space. The opportunity is there, and once you get used to it, you'll see it everywhere. The key lesson here is to spend as much time doing what you and your company do best and to delegate everything else that you can. This is true both because it's not profitable to do everything yourself and because, let's be honest, you're not that great at all those other tasks, are you?

If You *Can* Delegate, You *Must*

Here's another important leveraging principle we learned from David Maister: If you can delegate a task to someone else (or to a machine, for that matter) in order to save either time or costs, it is your duty to do so. Whether it's a matter of opportunity or straight-up dollars, the result is the same: If you can save your own time, then you should. We see this as an attitude toward life, because this is pretty much the only time we have, so why waste it away on something someone else can do? Business owners think this way, and so should you.

Something else happens when you delegate: The work you delegate (if you've done it smartly) gets better results. Think about your taxes. You *could* figure them out yourself, but if it costs only $100 for some online software, ask yourself: Which is worth more to you, your time or the $100? And what if the software can save you an extra $50 and all that time? What then?

Using Leverage to Build Dad-O-Matic

Chris has a very active and passionate community at chrisbrogan
.com. One day, he decided that he wanted to put together a blog
about being a dad, but because Chris loves collaborative projects,
he wanted to do more than just make a blog about how *he* acts as a
dad. He wanted a group blog, where dads (most of them with their
own blogs) would also contribute the occasional post about
parenting from a dad's perspective. That's how dadomatic.com
was born.

In less than 30 days, Chris had a blog with more than 50
authors, each passionate about the idea of writing about parenting. Guest contributors included famous evangelist and venture
investor Guy Kawasaki, top blogger Darren Rowse from Problogger
.net, and several dozen passionate dads from all walks of life.
The site was instantly stocked with great writers sharing
passionately.

The success of Dad-O-Matic all stems from how Chris leveraged his popular site, chrisbrogan.com, and his presence on
Twitter to reach out to dads interested in being part of a group
project with him. None of the dads had any financial reason to
join the project, and none of them were actively seeking more
writing gigs. And yet, because they knew having a relationship
with Chris would be fun and rewarding and that the project would
be successful, they joined in. Now the project is roaring along, and
people are reaching out to the dads of Dad-O-Matic to review
products, give opinions, and generally share a dad's perspective—
and it all came from moving energy from one successful project to
another. Others are also linking to the site from all over the Web,
which is giving it a boost in traffic and search engines normally
gained only by older and more established sites. That's the power
of leveraging a community toward a goal.

Wait, It Sounds Like You're Saying . . .

Yes, we are saying that the whole Web is one gigantic lever, and you can use it to accomplish pretty much anything more easily than before. That's because the Web is, by definition, technology, and using technology for leverage is one of the most fundamental ways we humans have gotten where we are today. Most people wait for technology to become common before they start taking advantage of it, but this is the kind of thing you should stop doing. Becoming an early adopter of technology sometimes means paying more, or putting effort into understanding a certain tool before there's a manual for it, but it also means you're there at the beginning, which leaves you in a better position than others when the technology is common, even connecting you with more business opportunities.

The real secret of the most successful people on the Web is that they are always trying new things. A lot of the time it's just for fun, because they are passionate about it and like to see how things work. But the benefit is that it's there for business, too. Early adopters always know more about what's coming up, and that leads to advantage, over and over again. The company that doesn't see how it should innovate will always lose over the one that knows how, because it leverages that information to domi-nate its marketplace. And so should you.

Finally, Why We Used Traditional Publishing

While we were working on the first draft of this book, we were asked repeatedly why we were going the way of a traditional publisher (in this case, John Wiley & Sons) instead of going the indie route. People were saying that books are dead (something we said about radio in early podcasting days, too), and we were hearing many examples of people going with small publishers, or using book services like Lulu.com for their publishing needs. In addition, both of us had published a number of e-books before, and the process was quick, effective, and fun. So we found ourselves on the phone one day, asking why we were choosing a real publisher instead of doing this on our own. Sure, publishing by ourselves would be more time-intensive, but the profit margins are higher and we'd have more control. Why, then, should we go with a traditional publisher? What was the point?

The phrase we came up with, which is admittedly crass but does hit the point home, is that we did it to "piggyback off the prestige of traditional publishing." After all, we could have sold a great number of books on our own, and the marketing budgets for first-time authors is never huge, so most of the marketing would be our efforts, anyway. But could we have convinced anyone that what we were doing was quite as important if we had just decided to do it ourselves? We didn't think so. There's something kind of exciting about having a book deal and a traditional publisher—to the nonwriting public, anyway—and we felt that it would give our ideas credibility in the outside world instead of just in our own little bubbles on the Web. As we once heard veteran author David Maister say, "A book is like a big, thick, impressive $25 business card."

Besides which, neither of us were really thinking about this book as a moneymaking venture in the first place. We'd been told a thousand times that writing a book for money is just not a smart thing to do. So, we took it for what it could give us: old-world credibility. We know that blogging and new media, while useful to us and to all the people we are in business with, just isn't as credible to the gatekeepers at the top of the hill. This book is our key—it fits perfectly in the lock, and we hear a nice big click when we turn it. It opens doors just wonderfully. Leverage.

5

Agent Zero

Why work at connecting with others? Why use social networks to reach out to colleagues and potential business partners? Our friend, Christopher S. Penn from the Student Loan Network, couldn't have said it better:

> Because the wider your net, the greater your opportunities.
> A large bank in California hit me up on Facebook on Wednesday. Their student loan provider went out of business. A friend of a friend referred them to me.
> Deal signed. The value: seven figures.
> Cost? Only the cost of maintaining the net.

Jim Canterucci, CEO and founder of Transitional Management Advisors and author of the book *Personal Brilliance*, said this about connecting:

> Practically, the answer to "why social media?" is about opportunity cost. Yes, we can get by without it, but what are we

missing when we aren't connected. Last week, I signed a business transaction that was facilitated exclusively on Twitter. I would have been fine in my ignorance. But, rather we now have this new business. Opportunity cost—what is possible?

Now, to the bigger question: Do we need the resulting innovation taking place in social media? Did we really need the printing press, the automobile, the television, the airplane?

If you really think about it, we could have gotten by without these innovations. We didn't really *need* product. But, what we do need is the process of innovation, the habit of creating new things and turning them into a practical application, to help fulfill our nature as humans.

Social media tools are no different. We don't really need the resulting innovation, but the process of generating the innovation encourages creativity and improves our capabilities.

It's Not Who You Know, It's Who Knows You

Our friend Mitch Joel, author of *Six Pixels of Separation*, used to say this in presentations. Trust agents have a natural tendency toward being the connector in all of their different groups. In their place of business, they work in positions that connect internal teams, external colleagues, and more. Online, they are the ones being asked for, and sending, frequent introductions via e-mail and through social networks. No matter where they go, trust agents have a desire to connect good people together. We refer to this as being Agent Zero; being in the center of a network and being able to spread ideas.

In Figure 5.1, Agent Zero is the link that connects one small group to another group.

How do trust agents do this? First, trust agents are naturals at finding other connector types in other groups. They are able to

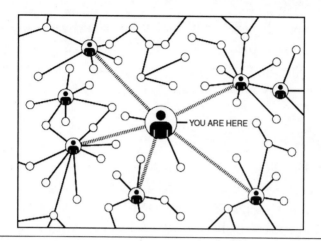

Figure 5.1   Being Part of Multiple Groups Helps Your Access Grow.

recognize the individuals who like building networks of value and know how to reach out. Second, trust agents who are connecting do this across almost all of their groups, constantly seeking ways to make their groups connect with each other. Thus, trust agents are also individuals who often blend their work group with their outside-of-work social group, and more.

A natural benefit of these tendencies is that trust agents often get the opportunity to meet influential people. As connectors like to network and reach others, so it seems that if they have a famous, strong, powerful, and/or useful connection, they are quick to share it. When making connections, it's important to understand how trust agents approach meeting someone who is considered famous or prominent in his or her social circle.

One of the best pieces of advice Chris received early on came from Steve Garfield of SteveGarfield.com. The two were sitting in Garfield's kitchen, which also happens to be the set of the "Steve & Carol Show," an occasional video segment Garfield records with his wife.

"People are people," he said. "Just treat them like someone you're meeting at work. Be polite, but don't gush." Learning to treat people right means remembering that at the end of the day we're all pretty much the same.

Agent Zero Connects the Web

Trust agents build networks almost reflexively by being helpful, by promoting the good work that others do, by sharing even their best stuff without hesitation, and by finding ways to deliver even more value on top of all that without asking for anything in return. Instead of sucking up to the big guys (which we've already mentioned isn't the right strategy), trust agents reach out to the up-and-comers. They make friends with the people starting out, those who might not be the big voices or the movers or the shakers, but who are interesting, driven, talented, and have potential.

How is this accomplished? First, efforts are made through several small touches online, such as commenting on people's blog posts, responding to their Twitter messages, or helping get the word out about their causes or efforts. Second, it's helpful to be able to meet some of the people you've built online relationships with.

Though the Web is loaded with tools to build and sustain online relationships to levels never before considered, cementing these relationships with a face-to-face event, be that a conference or just a beer or two at a local pub, is a powerful way to strengthen them even further.

The key to developing a solid network is first to build a presence online, then meet in person, and then sustain the relationship with several more online touches over time. This can include anything from e-mail to comments on each other's blog or podcast to just commenting back and forth to each other on social networks like Facebook or Friendfeed. Having had face-to-face personal contact tends to make the online relationship connection even stronger.

Personal networks are extenders, a way to reach into more places, a way to scale, an opportunity to have more than your own eyes and ears on a problem. They are the new resource for finding new jobs, new business opportunities, new anything. Trust agents can call upon their network to help solve a problem. They may need the help of someone who has skills or abilities outside their own. The other, less obvious, reason for this is that by sharing opportunities with their network, trust agents build even more social capital (see next section, "Agent Zero at Work"). Meeting new people, building relationships with them, and then having the ability to reach out to these people in a moment of need is a skill that trust agents rely on all the time.

Different levels of trust develop between people within these networks. When you go to Amazon.com to read reviews of a book or product, a certain level of trust is achieved simply by reading the review online. Previous visitors to a page rate these reviews, and this gives us some sense of its value. Within our own networks of people we know (or at least feel like we know), the level of trust is even stronger.

Though this should feel rudimentary, it's not. Why? Because we humans, by our very nature, can be greedy, and most business cultures only make that worse. The elements of network building are all about being helpful and forming new relationships that aren't built on quid pro quo requirements, and this can feel like you are doing something that's not necessarily in your nature to do.

As you connect more people together with beneficial outcomes, the level of your perceived trustworthiness goes up in the eyes of those you have connected. This allows you to build even stronger relationships with more people. It's a multiplier effect that becomes, in and of itself, a powerful asset for a trust agent to have.

Creating tangible results by helping someone is a great way for a trust agent to become Agent Zero and make the best kinds of relationships. The simplest way to do this is to promote good work. You can write about people doing great things on your blogs, talk about these people on social networks, or go out of your way to introduce good people who might find mutual business benefits from meeting each other. Trust agents do this without fanfare and without lingering around to show that they were the catalysts. You can also share lots of the business opportunities that come your way, handing them out to people who might be able to execute. There are only so many hours in a day, and sharing serves two purposes: (1) It means that you are helping others make money, and that alone is a great reason. (2) It means that people will think of you should an opportunity arise.

Agent Zero at Work

Businesses are starting to understand the value of having strong connectors on staff. The old way of doing business was to use the resources at hand within your company. Now, it's just as possible that you might reach beyond the borders of the organization to find information or to build a relationship that will help complete a task. It's not that you should share proprietary business information with external sources. We're not advocating that. But there are many instances where a potential business opportunity, or some piece of information important to a business, can be sourced through connections outside the company.

Sales organizations, for instance, can take great advantage of the way the Web helps a trust agent do business. Reaching out into other organizations is easier now that we have several mutual watering holes like Facebook, Twitter, and even newer platforms. We have found many occasions where, in the process of reaching out to find a source of information or a business opportunity, a social networking site is often the source of the solution to helping us achieve a goal. LinkedIn, for instance, and Xing, are great platforms to find people for various needs.

One example: Chris had an opportunity to speak at an event in Los Angeles. He would have enjoyed attending, but his schedule was booked. Instead of simply replying that he couldn't attend, Chris searched his LinkedIn contacts, narrowed the search to the Greater Los Angeles area, and then found at least 15 people who could potentially fill the slot. He sent the three most likely candidates in his e-mail reply to the person who'd offered the speaking engagement and thus provided an opportunity to someone else in his network.

There are two trust agent moves in this example. One was the Agent Zero effort of using one's network to solve a problem. The other was the Archimedes Principle of building leverage by giving someone else a business opportunity. Though it's a "nice thing to do," giving business to friends and sharing business opportunities through one's network is also very useful in the sense that it gives the recipients a sense that you have performed a valuable act on their behalf. This goes back to social capital, which we discussed earlier.

The process of becoming Agent Zero can be divided into a few steps, some of which you do online and others in person. First, you must build awareness of who you are, making people aware that you exist. Next, you try to grab their attention and have them see that you are a good person to know, because you are entertaining, informative, and/or useful. Then you take that recognition and develop it across several groups, to a level where you are considered an authority in as many of these groups as possible. Here's how it happens.

1. Awareness

Can humans be modified to detect magnetic fields? It had been discussed in body modification circles for years, but Todd Huffman, a graduate student at Arizona State University, was actually willing to find out by becoming the first to implant a magnet into his finger.

The original idea, conceived of by body modification artists Jesse Jarrell and Steve Haworth, was to have an implant carry metal gadgets with the magnet. But Huffman had a background in neuroscience. To him, the idea that he could obtain a new, strange sixth sense was fascinating. Once implanted, the magnet worked. Said Huffman of the experience:

> I have walked in and out of dozens of libraries hundreds of times, and never once have I thought about the magnetic fields passed through me to prevent people from stealing a book. I have been intellectually aware of the mechanism, but never paid attention until now. Another time I opened a can of cat food for my girlfriend's pets, and I sensed the electric motor running. My hand was about six inches away from the electric can opener, and I could feel where the motor was inside of the assembly. Again it brought my attention to a magnetic source that I always understood to be there, but would have otherwise been unaware of.[1]

---

[1] To read the whole story: http://www.wired.com/gadgets/mods/news/2006/06/ 71087.

We see stories like this popping up everywhere among the wide collection of science fiction books available, but these stories come from the real thing: individuals increasing the senses of their own bodies, purposefully or not, to include awareness of additional things around them. The people we call *digital natives* do this, too. The tools are limited, but their awareness of a wide collection of information increases every day, and with the emergent social Web, that awareness is coming to include a wide awareness of friends, colleagues, and coworkers all around the world.

There's *a lot* happening around us we don't know about. Sometimes it's simple: knowing glances between people at parties. Sometimes whole forces do their work in ways we aren't aware of, building an understanding of networks, social connections, and human behavior dynamics into our way of seeing things.

Becoming Visible

People tend to form networks naturally. All the social connections we make increase either the size of the network (by including new people) or its strength (by having those social ties become stronger). Trust agents try to do both.

With the rise of the Facebook generation, "What are you doing right now?" has become an omnipresent request, and accepting its call is the first way to make your presence felt. Like a billboard erected near a freshly built road, it may be a while before anyone sees these status messages, but if that road becomes a highway, that billboard will become the best investment of your life. And it all starts with taking a chance.

We won't lie: The decision to become visible is a risk. By choosing to have a web site when it doesn't seem profitable, you are taking a risk, although later, it may seem to have been the obvious choice. Likewise, building that billboard by investing either time or money into social media is chancy. But if you run a business, you're used to risk, and you know that taking risks can become a great advantage. When a company decides to "go social," there are concerns that are reasonable to have, and it's important to have several conversations before deciding to move forward.

Your First Status Message

Creating status messages may be done for personal reasons, but there's no hiding the fact that they appear in public and, consequently, make an impression on people. The public nature of all online activities makes it necessary to understand the impact you're having on both friends and strangers who read what you've left there.

One strategy to combat creating a very limited view of who you are is to try to leave many messages all over the place, from Facebook to Twitter to blog comments, ensuring you connect with a lot of people all the time, if only peripherally. It's the digital equivalent of "never eat alone," the mantra of author Keith Ferrazzi, whose book of the same title describes the maintenance and expansion of personal networks.

So, write a status message for yourself. Log onto Twitter, or create an account if you don't have one yet, and type something in. We suggest "Reading Trust Agents," because it's short, simple, and will let us know you're out there so we can connect. (Don't worry, we can find you.)

After you've done this, send something out again, maybe an hour or a day later. Make a habit of publishing your thoughts regularly. You'll thank yourself later as you look over them, or as you realize you've made an impact on the lives of others by making them laugh or helping them out.

I Am the Path

Our neural networks are constantly establishing new pathways as we learn about different concepts and ways to approach problems. Learning to ride a bike is a great example. As children, we don't know the process or have the motor skills to maneuver a bicycle, so it's unfamiliar and awkward. But as we develop the skills necessary to ride—pedaling, balancing, and eventually using no hands—our brains adjust. Soon, we are able to ride with ease. The thought process is still there, of course; it just becomes unconscious and the skills become ingrained. It's the same with research, human communication, information retrieval, or any other activity.

As with the neural pathways of our brains, so likewise with human networks and the Web: Our behaviors follow the patterns that work for us. If we want to know about medicine, we're likely to go to Wikipedia.org or WebMD.com, or to ask a friend who's a doctor. When walking through a neighborhood, we'll analyze the streets on our internal map for the most likely traffic-free route. But the process is always the same: We assess a variety of known options in order to find the best option for us, evaluating risk and reward along the way. The job of Agent Zero people is to place themselves among those routes, to become one of those options.

Like the billboard along the stretch of new highway, the cost of our resources is relatively small, but should the highway become a major thoroughfare, the reward is great. After the billboard has been erected (see preceding, "Your First Status Message"), we begin the process of placing ourselves at many intersections along many traveled paths. Of course, the most commonly used path to information is Google. We'll get to that later. Right now, we're dealing with human networks rather than informational ones.

Always Be There

While we were writing this book, Julien often went to a particular café to work on his laptop. He had a schedule. But one day he decided to move from the tables, which took up about 80 percent of the place, to the bar, where those waiting for tables hung out, and something happened. He had been seen around forever, so the regulars knew his face, but there seemed to be a shift in the waiters' perceptions: that somehow Julien's change in seating had improved their relationship. Maybe it was just being physically closer to them, maybe something else. But being aware of how to get closer, and the *right way* to do it, is a skill that takes practice.

Remember Donnie Brasco: When he was trying to infiltrate the Mob, before he tried to gain their trust, he needed to be seen. The reason for this was clear to him: People are trusted not only because they give signals of trust to others, but also because they do it over a long period of time, which is what Julien did with his routine. It works, because it shows regular behavior, and a person who has acted regularly in the past is seen as being likely to act the same way in the future.

The Web is very open to embracing new people, as long as they're not selling anyone anything. So, after you show up, be helpful (often by just not saying too much), and don't bother anyone by doing anything that's too self-interested (like Julien might have if he had started flirting with the waitresses). It's actually that easy. Social networking is not about getting attention for attention's sake, but rather about being a part of the network, making other people aware that you are there—and that you'll be there in the future, too.

Leaving a Trail

Regarding the Web as a new form of newspaper is a mistake. We live in a world that has gravity, weight, and mass, but the Web has none of these. Many don't realize what impact this lack of physical presence has, but when you start to see what your hours of Web surfing have amounted to, you begin to realize: If you leave no trace, no one will know you were there. You need to leave traces of your visits, markers on the trail, to show others that you have passed through.

By doing this yourself, other Web users are impacted. Their impression of you depends on what signals you leave, which is why a company with no Web presence has such a PR problem, displaying itself in an absence of involvement in a place many people find to be more of a home than their local tavern. As you now know, if you have no Google results, you don't exist.

The process of increasing awareness begins here: Create accounts in many places. Choose an official online name and stick with it for consistency. Never leave an empty, unused account anywhere, because it's as much an indicator of neglect as a dirty desk. Make the majority of your content conversational rather than solicitous, because it shows that you're genuinely listening and involved. With any luck, involved is what you actually will become (and, hey, that's the goal here).

How Not to Seem Like an Old-Fashioned Networker

We talk about the value of networking, but let's be clear: We're not talking about the old days, where you'd go to a cocktail mixer with a pocketful of business cards that you'd lob at passersby like a ninja hurling stars at victims. Nor are we referring to speed meeting, where you shake a few dozen hands, say "who-are-you-what-do-you-do-how-can-I-help-you?" over and over throughout the night. Get that out of your head. It's not what we're talking about.

Rather, trust agents build relationships where it makes sense to do so. They attend conferences that relate to their business interests and meet with people in the hallways, after sessions, or on the Web before the event, firming up relationships in person. They reach out to people in similar industries and approach these people as peers. They don't say hi just to say hi, but often have something of value to add to a discussion. Sometimes, they reach out to share a resource or to point out an opportunity for a new connection. There's always a plan of sharing a value first before seeking to gain anything from the relationship.

If you are the Agent Zero of your circle, it doesn't necessarily mean that you aren't shy, but maybe that you've developed a method by which you can get to know people easily. You understand the balance between being a "meet-everyone-in-the-room" old-fashioned networker and a "stick-to-one-person-as-if-you've-found-your-soul-mate-on-the-first-try" wallflower. It's good to meet a few people early on at an event (this could be a mixer, a meeting, or in the halls at a conference) and then proceed to take the opportunity to introduce these people to other parties of people as the opportunities arise.

Again, unlike old-fashioned networkers with a "what's in it for me?" attitude, trust agents are thinking strategically and considering opportunities for their newfound friends that are far downstream. If we meet individuals who are looking for a way to hire better people for their company, we think immediately of Ben Yoskovitz at StandoutJobs.com, who helps people build a better hiring process through video and more. If we meet someone who is visiting the United Kingdom on business and wants to meet with the Internet's brightest, we connect that person to Nico Flores at the BBC or Maz Nadjm at BSkyB, both great social media types who also know their way around London, for instance.

If you keep others' interests in mind while meeting people as a connector, you will build more opportunities for everyone as a trust agent.

2. Attention

Paying attention is difficult. People work more hours now than they ever have, and they spend more of those hours distracted than ever before, watching more simultaneous channels of infotainment than we ever imagined possible. If you're concerned about a shortage of oil or water, learn instead what activists and marketers have known all along: Attention is the scarcest resource of all. We now must face the fact that with thousands of cable channels and millions of personal channels on the Web scattered throughout the YouTubes and Twitters everywhere, everyone is in competition for your eyeballs, but you have less and less to give.

Who are you in competition with now? If your video store owners think they need to worry only about the new store down the street, they should think again. They have to worry about the competition on the Web and the fact that people now watch more 30-second videos than they do feature-length films. This deluge of institutional change is causing you to have to compete with *everyone for everything*. It's getting ugly.

The paradox is this: More channels, less focus, but somehow, you now need to pay attention to more of them to make sure you understand what people are thinking about you. This reality will impact your bottom line, and facing this daunting pandemonium of voices from all over the world can be intimidating. Which is one more reason to try to understand it all.

The other option is to ignore and put your head in the sand. If that's your style, feel free; it can be relaxing, for a while anyway. But information overload certainly isn't going away.

Happily, the tools that allow us to pay attention are the same ones that allow us to *develop* attention. They are two sides to the same coin, which, when put into the right machine, will unlock information you may never have known was available.

Channels and Subscription

Many of the terms in this book refer to concepts prevalent in new media, and that's because the Web is just another medium that sends and receives information, like other forms of media. A blog may or may not be a one-guy-and-his-dog affair, but whether a web site has a single reader or 100,000 readers, it's still a channel. We're in a world with infinite channels; a lot of them may not appeal to you, but so it is with anything else. You may like Animal Planet or you may not; the same is true of the Web and its personal channels.

Channel surfing may be an American tradition, but it's by far the most ineffective way to use the Web. A more effective model is *subscription*: This involves a small time commitment, and you can cancel at any time, but you need to subscribe or you'll fall behind. And falling behind on the Web is different than missing the next issue of *People* magazine, because it involves falling behind with people you ostensibly care about.

Our personal channels are in a constant state of flux: We may be amused, entertained, and informed by something, or not, and we can unsubscribe at any time, because it's usually a one-click process. So we subscribe *a lot*. The Web is a publish-then-filter environment, so by subscribing often, you're acting the way the Web itself does. It's easier to read too much and forget the stuff that didn't matter than to wonder what you're missing.

How to Decide What's Worth It

Infinite channels, limited time. What's worth watching? We're glad you asked. The way we figured all this out was through trial and error, but we also had an advantage: There were fewer blogs, podcasts, and other channels to watch when we first started, and catching it early helped us figure out the best methods, because that's what everyone was doing back then.

There are more channels now than ever before, so it may be more complex to wade through what's there. One strategy is to go through recommendations, which should feel natural to you since this is the way most people research restaurants, vacation spots, and everything else. It works like this: Find a channel you trust, watch it, and assess the differences you have between its opinion and yours. Follow recommendations that make sense, subscribe to those channels, and then continue the process from the root through to the branches.

When it comes to networks (Twitter, Facebook, whatever), learning where to stake your claim is a bit more complicated, because it involves a continuous commitment. One option is to start with whatever you find entertaining, but also to stake your claim in every network as a matter of principle to claim the username you prefer. This is how Julien got @julien on Twitter, for example, though he missed the boat on Identi.ca, another microblogging tool, and was relegated to @jules. Getting into the game early, committing *a few* resources, helps us be in a better position later, when we decide we want to get in deeper.

Trying New Stuff

Edward de Bono, Rhodes scholar, physician, author, and creator of the term "lateral thinking" has written a lot about creativity in his books, *Serious Creativity* and *How to Be More Interesting*, specifically focusing on the ability to be creative in a purposeful, methodical way. Using a thought mechanism he calls "Po" (short for *provocation*), he would ask people to work with a sentence such as, "Po: Cars have square wheels," which could lead to further ideas about how car wheels could be improved. (This method led to ways of improving shock absorption.) Try it out: Precede any sentence with the term "Po" and then refuse to be critical of the statement. This can lead to constructive, rather than negative, responses to an idea.

Being critical may be the most typical state for us to be in, but it certainly isn't the only one we have access to, nor is it the most productive (by far). De Bono proved, through his CoRT thinking system, that creativity mechanisms such as Po allow those who use them to come up with far more ideas than when they use no techniques at all.

The process of developing a wide network of attention can be approached in a similar way. The process of finding new, exciting, and profitable information is difficult, precisely because popularity of any one piece of information reduces its value. Imagine a huge sale at a department store: It's much better to get there before anybody else knows about it, because otherwise all the good stuff is gone.

When it comes to meeting people, many will dismiss the idea of attending an event because it isn't useful, without being aware of the opportunity cost of doing so (especially if the other option is to stay home). The idea of potential and opportunity cost can be applied to almost every aspect of your interactions with people, whether neighbors or business partners or anyone in between. Keeping in mind the notion of potential opportunities, it follows that any chance meeting can develop into a very fruitful relationship, so it becomes clear that giving up an opportunity to connect makes no sense. Having this mind-set, you will start to see opportunities in encounters as small as helping a neighbor carry groceries or heading to the garage sale down the street (though no one really ever finds anything at a garage sale). These opportunities are rarely financial, but that's just the point. You aren't building a network so that you can line your pockets, but rather because there are benefits of all kinds available to people who have a wide support structure of others they care about.

Anatomy of a Face-to-Face Meetup

More and more social gatherings are using the "meetup" model. These events are informal, usually take place at a bar or coffee shop, and often have a mix of business-minded professionals and as social connectors. Meetups are often sponsored events, but even this is often handled in a lightweight way. There's even a Meetup.com site, where you can learn if there are any events in your area, though many events happen without being facilitated through that site. What goes on at these events is interesting. These gatherings are important to the new way we do business.

Meetups are often not very conducive to business these days, and yet, by being there, people can see you (we talked previously about being visible), and you have opportunities to connect your online presence with face-to-face humans. There are some rules about how we prepare and conduct ourselves at meetups.

Before events, we can search for information about who may be there. By finding a list of people attending, or perhaps by their blogging URLs or their company affiliations, a trust agent can conduct searches. Check Flickr.com and see if you can find a photo of the vice president of marketing at BSkyB so you'll recognize him. Look at Twitter and see if you can find any reference of that person's company name. This preliminary work helps you learn more about the people who will be attending the event, what they're interested in, how they conduct themselves online, and perhaps even more.

At the event, make a point of finding the people you most want to meet earlier rather than later. Things happen. Moments pass. Sometimes, it's not easy to connect with the person you originally intended to meet with. If you can make the introduction early on, it's better than to risk missing that connection altogether.

As mentioned in the accompanying sidebar, it's not about how many cards you hand out; it's about how many useful cards you take in. Building up a pile of cards just to have them is useless. This isn't intuitive, and there's no harm in building your own personal database by collecting cards from people you meet, but unless you can somehow differentiate the "long-shot" cards in your stack from the "potential business" and "potential partner" cards, be wary of building fat databases from events.

At the event, never take up too much of any one person's time. Be polite, be conversational, be civil, and be interesting. Keep the topics you discuss fairly light, unless the other person is really pushing you to go deeper, or unless you won't have the opportunity to meet with this person again for some time. Don't drag out the conversation until you're both bored—excuse yourself early, instead. For chat time, we like to follow the 30-60-90 rule: For the first 30 seconds, they're listening to you; after 60 seconds, they may be distracted; after 90 seconds, it's really time to let them talk, too.

After the event, send a brief message to the person and, if there seemed to be potential business, ask for the meeting. If the conversation was even further along, don't be afraid to ask for the sale.

ACTION: The Business Card Game

Yes, business cards are *so* 1987, and yet, they are just as important today as they have been for the past several years. Don't dispute us. Just make sure you have business cards, whether or not your company supplies them. (There are many places to get them online: Moo.com, OvernightPrints .com, and VistaPrint.com are just a few.)

Here are some tips.

Card Design

- Have your name be the most visible element on the card, especially your first name.
- List your mobile phone number, your e-mail address, and your blog URL at the bare minimum.
- List your Twitter or other important social network IDs, if you want contact through those networks.
- Leave the reverse side blank for note writing.

Card Tricks

- Don't hand out cards like you're an automatic dispenser. In fact, ask for the other person's card first—and only if you want to make further contact.
- Offer your card only in return.

(continued)

(*continued*)

If you have another person's card, you can call back. If you've only given out yours, the ball is in the other person's court.

Thank people for their cards. They have committed an act of trust at that moment. And, if you were too shy to do it before, try to use that moment to make brief eye contact.

3. Influence

One of the 150

How many people do you know? How many times do you have to meet people before you remember their name?

The British anthropologist Robin Dunbar was the first to analyze the size of social networks in primates (like us) and to find the number at which it becomes difficult to maintain authentic relationships. That number hovers at around 148, so it's usually rounded off to 150. Malcolm Gladwell's *The Tipping Point* discussed how some people, whom he calls *connectors*, are the people who can be counted on to be known by anyone. They are the social butterflies, the restaurant owner of the most popular spot in town or the priest whose church everyone attends.

It seems to be a commonly held assumption that talent is the way to success for most people. There's a real myth out there trying to convince us that "if we're not born with it, we can't get it." We think it's a lie. You may not be a born connector, or you may be shy around people. So what? You can still teach yourself to be a connector and to be one among the 150 in your group—or in any group. It doesn't take a miracle; it takes some leg work and the right venue.

Be the Priest; Build the Church

In smaller towns, everyone knows each other (and all the gossip), but it is usually the priest who really knows everything. Churches aren't just about religion; they're also about creating wide opportunities for social exchanges and for allowing a wide network to develop. The priest is at the center of it all, able to take care of spiritual needs of a congregation and to grease the social wheels when grumpy neighbors are arguing over whose bushes are creeping over whose fence.

Churches help community members create a network of people to count on. The members see each other every weekend and help carpool to softball games. On a sociological level, it's a subtle structure of consistent, small sacrifices that allow everyone to know they have someone to count on, because they all helped each other last week, and the week before that, and so on, back as far as they can all remember. They stay together because these collective sacrifices have shown that people will be there for each other in times of need.

On the Web, we don't have churches, but we do have gathering places. Unlike churches, they are never designated "official" by some outside source, so we're never told by a central authority what the focal point should be. Instead, the decisions are bottom-up, rendered by the people who use them. Two challenges are important to recognize here: (1) How do you figure out what kind of church your community needs? (2) When you build it, will they come? No authority from on high is telling us where to go on Sunday (and many people would rather check out PostSecret.com than church), and decisions are made by individuals, which then trickle upward to form a sort of collective consensus about what the community wants. That consensus spreads through the group as a kind of authority.

Name-Dropping 2.0

There really are two reasons to mention the name of someone you know: One is for the effect of seeking external status by association. This is the more common way we observe people dropping names. We think it's kind of cheap. The other is to build association with someone who might benefit from the association with you. The latter opportunity works well for the trust agent and for the person being mentioned.

Another way you could look at this is to call it *praise*. Chris says that Jon Swanson is a thoughtful blogger and pastor. Julien says that Clarence from DoYouKnowClarence.com is a great storyteller. When this is said "on paper," as we've mentioned elsewhere, it has the added effect of helping others discover the great work of Jon and Clarence and to show them that we're talking about them. Again, we wouldn't want to praise someone we don't endorse, so this transaction occurs because we want people to know about the good work of others.

By repeating this experience with many people in a network, a trust agent reinforces the larger network as a whole. Suddenly, Jon knows about Clarence, and Clarence finds out about Liz, and everyone knows enough about each other to visit their blogs, comment on Friendfeed, and share information on various other platforms on the Web. By blogging, commenting, linking, and creating even more connections between each other, Google and the rest of the Web start to realize these relationships as well. This also has the effect of building a network of trust that even computer algorithms, through Web links, start to recognize, understand, and promote for us.

Be the Relationship before the Sale

Greg Cangialosi, CEO and founder of Blue Sky Factory, said this to us one night in a small resort bar in Arizona:

> I met you both at PodCamp, and I didn't ask for anything. In fact, I gave you money by sponsoring the event. I hung out. I met all kinds of people, and I didn't ask for anything in return. A little while later, you end up using my product. You like it. And for the last several years, if someone asks you what they should use for e-mail marketing software, you mention me. I think the key to that is being in the relationship before the sale.

Cangialosi is talking about something called *status quo bias*, and he's absolutely correct. His model, while not exactly something marketers and salespeople can easily sell to the senior team, worked exactly the way offline word of mouth usually works. The difference is that we're all connected. Cangialosi's network grows by association with our networks, and these networks reach out into other places. Because Cangialosi knows to build relationships with clients before trying to sell them something, he creates not only customers, but evangelists.

By being there, by being One of Us, and by connecting with circle after circle of friends in a genuine way, Cangialosi leveraged his relationship into being our default answer for a good e-mail marketing platform provider. Becoming the default, or part of the environment, or the first name that comes to mind when a prospective customer thinks of X, is the longer-term goal. How do you get there? Earn the relationship.

Bring People into the Circle

In the newer world of the Web, and in the ensuing business relationships that this culture promotes, trust agents are all about inclusive relationships. People working in this space collaborate, they connect, they build business relationships without asking for outright favors or payment. Trust agents build networks, then build circles, and then include others in those circles.

The value of bringing people in is the value of expanding the potential of the network overall. It's a simple effect. It's not far afield from Surowiecki's *Wisdom of Crowds*, where having more than one voice adds to the experience. But in this case, more opportunities exist, because the new people added to the circle have their own groups and capabilities. Add to this the notion that Agent Zero is also spanning multiple circles and you see how simple it can be to build networks.

Relationships at Scale

Developing relationships in person is an easy task. When you're surrounded, you know it, and when there's a crowd, the volume gets louder. You get feedback easily. The challenge of relationships on the Web is that often this feedback doesn't exist on *either side* of the fence. This means you don't know how many people want your attention because you don't see the usual signals; in addition, no one who wants your attention knows, either.

We call this the "why didn't you answer my @#$%ing e-mail" syndrome. We know—it's catchy.

It's happened to everyone at some point. Even if you're just sitting under a pile of e-mail that is work-related and can't tell what the priority of each message is, it can get complicated. When you scale that and bring it to a worldwide audience of possibly tens of thousands of people, all of whom want a piece of advice about, say, how to monetize their blog, it becomes a veritable, never-ending deluge of communication. Not responding to all your e-mail leaves people feeling slighted. What happens when you receive messages more quickly than you're able to respond?

If this is where you find yourself, the first thing that needs to happen is a willingness to address the problem (sounds familiar, right?). Making a public issue of it without sounding like a martyr lets people know what you're dealing with and that your response might take time. It also makes them appreciate that you're aware of them. If you're looking for another tip, try the one-sentence response: "How, exactly, did you want me to help with this?" This gets the e-mail out of your inbox and puts the responsibility for the next communication on the individual who is asking for help. It's just a delay, but it helps make progress.

Addressing the issue of one-way intimacy is also important. This means tons of people know who you are, but you don't know a lot about them. You're on their radar, but they're not on yours. While this is a good problem to have, as far as things go, it can still be difficult and lead to hurt feelings. One way that we deal with this is to genuinely ask about people whenever we meet them face-to-face or communicate with them online. Chris tries not to talk about himself, but rather to give the stage to the other person. By working to ensure that interest has been displayed, it helps alleviate some of the unhappiness of another person feeling unknown or unimportant.

The rule of "multitouch" is important here. Send out small messages. Comment on blogs. Leave notes on Facebook or Flickr or wherever your community spends time. By reaching out and keeping relationships warm, opportunities flow more freely. If you're not working to maintain your network, it dwindles and shrivels up from lack of use.

Tips for Maintaining the Network

This chapter talks about the trust agent's strategy of being part of several "150" networks. You can connect and be the connector across several groups, such that you become the "known good" in several circles of friends and colleagues. As you might imagine, this takes work, and once you reach a certain-sized system of personal networks, new challenges will arise.

Basic touch. One component of maintaining your networks is to send out brief personal messages to check in with the individuals within your network regularly. As you develop more relationships, this becomes more difficult. One way to address this is to set reminders in calendars or your contact management database designating when you last spoke with a contact, and then set a ping reminder in a calendar application for you to check in with that person within a certain time frame.

Level of service. The amount of deeper connections that one trust agent can manage is finite. It's just part of being human. Plan up front by being careful not to set expectations that you can't manage once your circle or community reaches a certain size. If you're in a corporation, introduce more trust agents to spread the experience and value to others. Dell did this well by expanding outward from Lionel Menchaca to Richard Binhammer to Bruce Eric Anderson to several other quality trust agents, making the job easier for everyone.

Friends first. Through maintaining online a lot of relationships, it often happens that new and unknown people will come into the picture. As this happens, make sure you find ways to keep your friends visible. On social networks, use grouping functions to keep a view of your friends. On services like Facebook, keep attentive to the birthday function. Add these to your main calendar application, with alarms. Be sure to celebrate your friends' victories.

Raise armies. We discuss this more later, but building discipleship inside or outside of your company is important once you reach a certain scale. We both make an effort to maintain relationships with people who can do what we do (or some portion of it) so that when too much work comes our way, we can shunt this to people similarly qualified who might have more time. This won't play as well in a corporation, but perhaps there's an internal version. Frank from Comcast built out more people who could do what he did once he hit a critical mass of social media customer service work.

There are no shortcuts to maintaining relationships, but by using some of these methods, it's a little more likely that you can stay abreast of your friends and closer colleagues, so that you can keep networks alive and preserve your value as the trust agent working within several networks.

You Live or Die by Your Database

This section discusses your own personal database of connections, the representation of your personal network in a searchable form. Even if you're a cog in a corporate machine, if you're not in the business of building your own database of contacts, then you have to start. Now.

Chris learned this from the visionary Jeff Pulver, serial entrepreneur and seed investor and also the co-founder of Vonage. Pulver ran the wildly successful VON[1] conferences for more than a decade, and, although the events' business relies heavily on a contact database to market, Pulver kept his own personal database away from the corporate platform. The lesson, Pulver told Chris at the time, was that one's personal database was an asset as valuable as gold, if nurtured and maintained.

This doesn't require complex software (though there are several great applications that can help improve your database's usefulness). Something as simple as a spreadsheet with the right information is a great start. What should go into a personal database? Here are some basics:

- First name
- Last name
- Title
- Company
- E-mail
- Phone number (preferably cell phone)
- URL
- State/province where you reside
- Notes (could include several fields, depending on how you want to build the platform)

Beyond these basics, there can be all kinds of fields to slice information in different ways. For instance, what if you want to recall who you know in Manchester, United Kingdom, who works in the technology field and is currently employed? Beyond the aforementioned fields, you can also add an "Employed?" field and an "Industry" field. Determining the appropriate fields is a matter of anticipating how you may need to sort the information later, measured against how much data entry and management you're willing to take on.

There are several online applications that people use for contact management. Some use their Gmail account. Others use Plaxo. Still others consider LinkedIn a great place to store professional information. Software built specifically for contact management includes Highrise from 37 Signals, BatchBook from BatchBlue Software, and beyond that, there are several other applications. These are all great, and each has its benefits and drawbacks.

Using a database application *and* storing a local copy of your database at all times on your computer in a CSV (comma separated value) format is the safest and most effective method of storing contacts. Why? Because you can never fully trust that your database online will be accessible, that your account will stay up, and that your data or account won't become corrupt. To us, storing a local copy ensures that you control the database at all times. If, as we say, you live or die by your database, why would you trust a third party with its ultimate integrity?

Care and feeding of a database is another matter entirely. It takes a little work, but the results are stellar. Start by building your own database of information and get it into an application. Then, save a copy onto your computer to work with further. We promise that once you get a better sense of using your database, you'll experience the benefits quickly.

But here's an important caveat: *Don't be a collector.*

In building these social circles and spanning yourself across these various groups of 150, there is a negative tipping point where networking for the sake of networking overwhelms the value of your effort to be Agent Zero. In social networks, this is easily observed in profiles where people have high "friend" counts without any apparent reason, or such that the person's "friends" don't count for much in a business sense.

4. Reputation

Establishing a reputation is what happens when people start talking about you when you're not around. What do people say about you when you're gone?

The Web Speaks for You

A mass of Web content means that, eventually, the amount of work you *have done* is far greater than the work you are *currently doing*, and what happens with the Web is that, often, the stuff you used to do will count more than what you currently are working on. Google is a big part of this: Google finds the stuff that's already happened, not the cool new stuff, so you have to make sure that whatever it finds is solid. In a way, the Web is like your Hollywood agent: It speaks for you whenever you're not around to comment.

Julien encountered a problem with a newspaper because he hadn't fully recognized the impact of this. An absolutely awful picture someone had taken of him and posted on Flickr was the first result whenever people searched for his name, so when a newspaper needed a picture quickly, it chose that one, broadcasting this awful picture to his whole home city. It's a minor problem, but one that illustrates the severity of what else could happen. For example, journalists could find outdated information on your blog that is no longer valid. We're still in a world where what's printed is taken for granted as being true, so making sure you show people what they should see is always a challenge.

Still, we can learn a lot from this process. Reputation management is a burgeoning field right now because the process of checking everything is so daunting that large companies often need entire smaller companies to deal with it. For the most part, though, we don't think you'll need them; you can use some basic tools instead.

Six Tools for Reputation and Competition Management

1. Google Alerts: Does regular searches on any keyphrase. You can set up alerts on your own name, your usernames, and more. Julien used this with the phrase "canada bank crash" in late 2008 to find out whether his bank would go under (it hasn't, yet).

2. Rank Checker: Anything that checks rankings in Google will do. Google is a good representation of the current zeitgeist on any subject, so this tells you how people are starting to view you. We like Aaron Wall's Firefox plug-in, available at tools.SEObook.com.

3. Technorati: An oldie but a goodie. Check how well you're doing in terms of links from bloggers—and how prominent those bloggers are. Another way of telling who's talking about you, but only when they link. You can also use Google Blog Search.

4. Compete.com: Nobody uses Alexa anymore. How's your traffic doing in relation to others in your field, and where is it coming from? Compete buys data from ISPs, so it has a great idea about how everyone is doing.

5. Twitter Grader: This is like ego surfing. Who are the Twitterati in your area? How well are you doing compared to the rest of the crowd?

6. Search.Twitter.com: Real-time representation of what digital natives are talking about at any time.

Links as Currency

To trust agents, hyperlinks are the twenty-first-century equivalent of the name-dropper. Seeing your link on someone's web site means that you have caught their attention, that you're on their radar, and traffic is one of the measurable ways of gauging the influence of a would-be trust agent.

Julien has a tendency of hyperbolically saying that anything that isn't a link doesn't matter. Being recognized by the mainstream press does wonders for clients' egos, but it delivers absolutely zero in terms of conversions, new readers, or attention if there's no link on their web site. Pretty upsetting, especially considering the cost of PR.

One reason for this is because there's a lot of drop-off of readers between one medium and another. Of the 100 people reading a Web page, maybe 5 percent will click that one link that leads to your web site, leading to maybe one subscription or sale. But the rate of distraction *between* media is much higher, and the likelihood of someone reading about your project in the newspaper and then heading over to your site is extremely low. Even considering that a print publication has many more readers, the actual increase in visits is minimal. We've seen this with magazines, newspapers, mentions in podcasts or videos, and so on. We have one example where the subscription rate to a particular YouTube channel has hovered at 6,000 subscriptions per 3 million views (or 0.2 percent). Not exactly the best ROI.

Does this mean that there is literally *no value* in mainstream press? Not really. It has more to do with the niche that you're in, and remember that, if you're working with the Web, getting an article in your local paper really won't do much, as great as it at first seems. This perception has something to do with the way we've been brought up, thinking that being mentioned in a newspaper somehow meant that you'd "made it." But this isn't the case at all; it's more likely to mean that a journalist had a deadline than anything else.

If you're able to make it in the niche you are actually involved in, what mainstream press does mean is that you will gain mindshare among other people in that niche. Being mentioned repeatedly in the local paper may get you coffee at your breakfast place faster, but how that translates can be difficult. If you live in a town full of bloggers and Web aficionados, then this local mindshare might result in more mentions on the Web. If articles are published often, you may become a resource for future articles. But there isn't necessarily any crossover there. It's hard to make the leap from Web to mainstream, or vice versa, unless you're catching a rising trend.

Links mean something else entirely to search engines, like Google. They look at certain of the Web's signals to give them an idea of what relationships there are between two sites. Google's proprietary ranking mechanism works a little bit like this. It infers relationships based on the number of links to a page and the importance of those links. If site A has 100,000 links and site B has only 1,000, we can deduce that site A must be better known.

The important thing to know is that *links infer relationships*. The more links your site has (from good sources), the more popular Google thinks it must be, and likewise with every site you get a link from. If you have 10 links from pages that have 10,000 links *each*, that's generally better than having 1,000 links from sites with no links going into them, because those no-link pages are basically nobodies. (Incidentally, this is what link spammers do, and that's why some blogs need comment spam protection.)

If we look at it in black-and-white terms, the lesson here may be this: For success on the Web, it's better to have a few connections that link to you *on the Web* than a lot of connections that mention you off the Web. That stays true even if the mentions are in generalist, mainstream press. You should strive to receive mentions from online sources *with* links and to use offline sources without links (generally those same, big, mainstream publications) to prove to those who don't know better how amazing you are. But we know the truth: No links? Doesn't matter.

How Trust Agents Use LinkedIn

We didn't really intend to discuss specific tools in this book. One reason is that these tools will change on a regular basis. The other reason is that we're saying that the human stuff is far more important than the software. It's understandable that the tools can be overwhelming, but those aren't the real meat of what trust agents work with. Use the tools that work to reach the people you need. Use them well, but know that they're just tools.

All this to tell you about LinkedIn.

LinkedIn.com is a site that helps people manage their professional identity on the Web. It allows people to enter resume-like information, and that's where most people seem to stop using the tool. Either that or they'll "friend" a few coworkers. Beyond that, it's hard to know what to do next. Here's how trust agents look at LinkedIn.

LinkedIn is a living network of relationships, and it is a reputation engine. It's the opportunity to connect with people and build business relationships. LinkedIn can be used a little differently than the company prescribes. The site suggests that you should connect only with people you have met and built strong relationships with. But LinkedIn can be used as a tool to capture the potential of the human network, and you can link to people within your social circle, people you know by reputation, and people you feel are good business connections to have.

One very important point: Though you can connect to people you don't know well, you should not recommend someone you couldn't vouch for personally. One of the hidden gems within LinkedIn is its reputation management function. Stay very pure on this. If someone takes your recommendation about someone you can't truly vouch for, what does it say about your own reputation?

Finally, ask for recommendations from business professionals who have worked with you in some capacity. Don't be afraid to ask for them, and, if you can, return the favor. These recommendations make for a powerful social proofing and mean a great deal to how others perceive your LinkedIn profile's overall value. Think of it as the classic third-party pitch. It's better to have someone other than you tell people how great you are.

ACTION: Get LinkedIn

Dust off your LinkedIn.com profile. Refresh it and start connecting to potential business partners, prospects, and friends. Here are some first steps:

- Rewrite your profile to highlight your current capabilities and future business interests.
- Add a candid (versus stuffy corporate) head shot.
- Start finding colleagues and connecting.
- Solicit connections on your less formal networks, like Facebook, Twitter, or the newer networks.

---

5. Authority

Proper self-definition, as discussed in Chapter 2, "Make Your Own Game," is the key to authority in a niche. Define yourself as a productivity guru, and you'll find yourself competing with Merlin Mann at 43folders.com, and Leo Babauta of ZenHabits.net. But be more specific and say you're an "e-mail workflow productivity expert," like Jared Goralnick of AwayFind.com, and you won't compete with any of them. (We call Jared that; that's not what he'd say about himself, probably.) Further, if you sell a product, your audience, although smaller, will probably be more targeted and more likely to buy from you. We don't know which you would rather be, but as business owners, we'd prefer not to be shooting blindly at a general, untargeted audience 90 percent of the time.

How We Use the Web for Authority

Human beings can't make individual decisions about everything they do, so they often go about asking authorities about the "right decision" in any given situation. For example, if we need to clean our shoes, we'll ask Google how to do it, since we know nothing about the subject. This is how, at the very last minute, Julien learned to tie a necktie (this was last year, if you can believe it). This is a conscious example, where someone deliberately decides they don't know how to do something, but there are other kinds of decisions made by authorities, too, where we think a decision is ours, or where information has been internalized, though we have no evidence of it. We'll repeat the information as if it were ours, but in fact, we just got it from "a reputable source." Rumors often spread this way, and only rarely does checking the actual evidence come into play (President Obama being a "secret Muslim" comes to mind).

The process of becoming an authority is often just a matter of triggering a person's filters. Make things seem credible enough, and people won't check them. Numbers generally do this quite convincingly, which is probably why we claim the three kinds of lies are "lies, damn lies, and statistics." We believe that the process of becoming an authority should be a practice of not only building a network that listens, but also being the best resource available. Empty demagogues aren't wanted here, and furthermore, you'll be discovered very quickly.

Two Types of Authority

As mentioned earlier, Julien learned how to tie a necktie from Google. This type of information doesn't require a lot of authority to accept. If the tie looks similar to the information provided in the instructions, then the information is good enough.

But what if you want help in deciding which wine to purchase. You might want to know more about the reputation and the authority of the person recommending the wine. We mentioned Gary Vaynerchuk, who runs Wine Library TV, where he gives his impressions of the taste, quality, and value of a few different wines during each episode. With tens of thousands of viewers and hundreds of thousands of visits per episode, it's safe to say that the Internet provides visual proof that Vaynerchuk's opinion is respected and heeded (for the most part).

The first example is indicative of anonymous authority. It's information that you need, but the value of the source isn't as important. The second example relates to trusted authority, where you want to know about the provider of the information so that you can decide whether to value the opinion you receive. Understanding what goes into defining authority on the Web, and how people can see visual signs (social proof) of this authority, is what becomes important next.

Social Proof: The Coffee Shop Example

Social proof is what happens when people attempt to gain cues from other people about how to act or react in ambiguous situations. For instance, if you and a friend are out walking in Paris after dinner, and you wander down the Rue de Buci, what if there are five cafés looking for your business? Four of the five have absolutely no customers, and the fifth has such a crowd that the line is out the door. People are stuffed into the place, waiting in line, and looking very happy to be there. Which café would you visit?

Most people's answer would be the busy one, because clearly there's something wrong with the other four shops. Is that what you answered? If you thought differently about it, did you at least wonder what caused one café to be more important than the others?

Social proof on the Web encompasses all those signs that point to a person's authority in the Web world. Let's look at other examples.

Social Proof: Online Examples

Visit someone's blog and you'll see details such as how many comments a post received. You'll be able to use a service like Compete.com to measure how many monthly visits the site gets. You can use tools like Technorati.com to determine how many other sites link to this one. These are examples of social proof in action.

Others include visiting people's Facebook profiles to determine whether they have a well-written profile, with a picture and enough information to prove they're human, or checking Twitter or some of the newer networks to see whether someone has "friends" there.

Seeing the quality of people's LinkedIn profiles gives another point of proof. Do they have recommendations? Have they filled out the form in a way that gives you a strong perspective on the quality of their work? Have others engaged in any form or function?

It's an interesting part of understanding how to decide to trust someone you know only online. It's not a science, but it's one of the ways people use to form an impression of someone they do not interact with face-to-face.

What's Next?

So much has been said about networks, but networks are made up of individuals. Keep reading if you'd like to figure them out. We have a lot to share.

6

Human Artist

What if Etiquette Isn't a "Nice to Have" Skill?

The balance of power within company-to-customer relationships has changed. Companies have had a great run from the 1950s to the early 2000s. Consumers devoured media and extra helpings of advertisements. We accepted that companies we patronized offered exactly what we needed. We nodded our heads. But those days are over.

Today, it's the consumer's world, and even in business-to-business land, the buyer is always in the better position. We have an infinite supply of goods and services looking for our consumption. There are seemingly endless possibilities and ever-increasing standards and demands. And when we are less concerned with quality, we just don't care enough to need to know. It makes for a strange place to consider business relationships. That's where etiquette comes in.

In the days when mass communication and pure advertising were all the rage, or at least the norm, etiquette was something used only by actors, copywriters, and the HR department. Look at your company's employee performance reviews. Is there anything there about etiquette? Maybe it's hidden in the company code of conduct. Are you familiar with that document? You get to read it and sign it every year in the bigger companies. It's something that senior management writes, usually with external forces, and that you're told to read, absorb, embody, and never cross.

In social media, human is the new black. People are the next revolution, and being active on the human-faced Web is your company's best chance to grow its business in the coming years. Sure, you can strong-arm. Sure, some companies don't need to care what their customers think. But for the rest of you, the ones operating in areas where a lot of choices are available to consumers, mark our words: Etiquette and understanding how to navigate this human Web are your best bets at finding, retaining, and growing communities of customers.

Look at it this way: There's a tidal wave coming, and it's made of people. Some will run and some will ignore it, but others will be ready and find a way to roll with it. Those who win are the ones who are always prepared; while some people are hiding their heads in the sand, the winners are anticipating change and finding a ton of opportunities. You can be a one of them.

Of course, for every little scrap of opportunity that the Web offers, there are land mines aplenty in this new, blended Web. It has been said that the Web is different from all other media developed over the past 50 years, and that's because it wasn't created for advertisers and commercialism. Newspapers, radio, TV, and even movies were fashioned around that. The Internet was conceived to enable scientists to communicate more fluidly with each other, and now we *all* can. The new Web still adheres to that fact: It's not built just to be a commercial endeavor. And that little truth has laid waste to many a company that has missed the mark in providing what its diverse audience needs.

Your key skill requirement: learning how to interact on your audience's terms. If you are to learn how to be a trust agent, the skill of being a Human Artist—someone who understands how to communicate with people in a real and thoughtful way—is very important to what you're doing. And with that comes a manifesto of sorts.

A Micromanifesto from Us Digital Natives

We both run businesses, sure, but we're also just a couple of guys who love the Internet. When we take off our business hats, this is how we think as Web *users*.

We both have short attention spans, but it's not because we're stupid or because we're from "that generation." It's because, like many out there, we have infinite channels to look through, with ever-increasing information about supposedly amazing things, but we have just as much time as the next guy. So we skim. Often. Because we're looking for good stuff that will help us personally.

We were born multithreading. We never focus on anything directly. And we're not even the apex. We're over the hill. Kids (17, say) watch TV like this: Forward to specific moments of a show using TiVo, while IM-ing with a friend who knows where the "good stuff" is, while texting another friend who's out with her parents, while doing homework.

If your new project didn't catch us, we're sorry, but that's not our fault. It's yours. We're just out looking for something to interest us, to entertain or inform us, in the little time we have between commuting, work, spouse, kids, and friends. We're looking for an edge for our web site or a laugh between very difficult sales calls. The options are to be a part of that or get out of the way. When you're in traffic, you have a purpose, and that's to go home: We have one, too, so please align yourself with what we want.

As bloggers, we're not interested in your press release. We're looking for something that'll interest our audience or, even better, our blogger friends who will link to us or at least notice. We don't usually find that with dry business copy, because no one has made the effort to try to appeal to us; they've just repackaged something (sometimes not even that) and expect it to stick. That is the "throw crap at the wall" strategy. Your prospects can tell when you make an effort and when you don't.

When we talk trash about your company and there's no one online representing you, it doesn't help your cause. However, if you are there, and you interact thoughtfully, then we realize that and tend to be more careful, because it's easier to trash someone who isn't around than someone we know is listening. So, just being online and accessible solves a lot of problems.

While we're on the subject, we interact with each other as a community of like-minded people, and that's the way you should respond to us, too. If you communicate with us the way you would with a company, you've missed the boat, and we tend not to be forgiving. Our first impressions of you strongly resonate with us on an emotional level, so they stick around for a while (and they stay on the Web forever). Take some time to think about how you want to do this before doing it, because that impression will last.

We know, this can be intimidating. It may not look like it, but everyone actually feels like that wallflower at the high school prom. They're intimidated about talking to strangers or asking someone to dance. But those who succeed tend to be the ones who *allow themselves to fail.* And, hey, if you don't ask for the dance, someone else will. You'll have missed your chance.

The Friends Thing

Social networks may call two joined user profiles "friends," but you know the huge difference between a Facebook friend and a "move my couch" friend. There's a lot to unfold here. But an important point is this: If you are trying to use the Web to sell, making friends with someone doesn't equate to becoming a prospect. It is essential to understand the difference, or you'll find yourself without either friends or prospects very quickly.

- Becoming friends means we've accepted your network connection. It means we're at least curious about who you are.
- Consider "friends" to mean that you can pay attention to what we're doing, and try to find a conversational entry point.
- Marketing to a new friend will almost always result in unfriending—and possibly an angry blog post.

It's simple: This is like saying hi at a party to someone you don't exactly know. It's a good start, but what you say next is probably more important.

The Basic Stuff

When you meet someone new, you shake hands, and when you do, you look each other in the eye. These are rules you learned along the way, rules that have existed for a long time. But there are digital equivalents on the social Web. Learn to play by the rules. People will notice and respond similarly.

It's easy to understand the online equivalent to etiquette by imagining that you're at a party where you don't know anybody very well. We'll use that analogy a few times here. Now, imagine that you have to be very deliberate about every gesture, because, as we've said before, with fewer social cues in online interactions, intentions can be gleaned only by your online exchanges. Here are some actions that should help make your experiences online more effective:

- **Listen.** The number one mistake newcomers make when they first begin their online experience is by diving in deep and stumbling over all kinds of social norms before they've realized any of it. "Lurking" simply means *listening*. If you're going to start reading blogs, pay attention to the way others comment. See how others respond to those comments. What's acceptable? What looks sketchy to you? Listening (i.e., reading what others are saying) before you make your first moves helps. A few days may often be enough time, but *you* decide when you're comfortable.

- **Ask.** If you are uncertain of what's acceptable and what's not, it's perfectly fine to ask people, provided you've spent a little bit of time in an online setting. Don't wander in and ask people to start at the beginning, but if you've listened a bit, you'll sense whom you might ask for helpful advice. Just remember, everyone started somewhere.

- **Reciprocate.** In real life, people may exchange pleasantries inadvertently, just because they're both there. Not so much online. All conversation happens on purpose, because we go to places purposefully, but we never communicate just because someone is there. When someone friends you (see "The Friends Thing" sidebar) on a social network, unless you have real reasons not to, friend them back. It's natural and it is the first step to opening a channel.

- **Comment and comment back.** When you are first getting started online, you can begin by simply being a visitor to the various online hangouts. Or by reading some blogs. Or by setting up a Facebook account. What comes next is *contributing*. Your comments should go beyond just saying "great post." Try adding to the conversation. Tell the author how his or her post relates to your business, or how you see things differently. If *you* are running a blog, do the reverse. If someone takes time to comment, comment back on his or her response. At the very least, drop an e-mail and thank the person. However you can, accept that comment as a first contact, and touch back.

The Golden Rule Ports Nicely to the Web

The manifesto of the Web user is important, because so many people involved in marketing have forgotten how to deal with people. ROI, click-through rates, and other statistics have become so important that sometimes we forget that, on the other side of these numbers, people are being impacted. And that's understandable. Back when all we needed was to throw more advertising on television to increase sales, it became a matter of tweaking copy or changing the color of the car in the ad in order to increase the response rate. Numbers have always been how effectiveness is tracked. But now everyone has a channel and, as small as some may be, any can be promoted to the front of Digg or any other popular blog and impact thousands of times its original readership. Because of this, every person with a channel is a possible Agent Zero. And we start to treat human beings as people once more, because it's the smart business decision to make.

As it turns out, the more we treat people the way they want to be treated, the better they react. How this happens on a group level is discussed in Chapter 3, "One of Us," but the core of human interaction is still a one-on-one relationship, and it's something we need to examine. After all, we've all had years of experience dealing with traditional interpersonal relationships, but only those individuals who are particularly aware, daring, or just don't give a damn end up interacting online and getting the hang of it. The rest hang back, wondering if they'll ever understand whether they should accept a friend request from a stranger and, if so, under what circumstances.

As Mark Hurst proclaimed in the productivity book *Bit Literacy*, we naturally understand how to deal with information in its analog format (as opposed to digital, like stuff on a hard drive) because it's real and sits there in piles on our desk. But we've never learned to deal with the bits, or core pieces, of information of the digital world, because we didn't grow up with them. We've had to adapt, and only those particularly capable were able to do it without any guidance, which is why most people end up with hundreds of unread e-mails in their inbox, wondering how in God's name it got this bad. In fact, they were just never taught *how*.

The same hurdles exist with online relationships. In face-to-face interactions, we receive all sorts of signals telling us how we're doing. We might get a kick under the table at dinner to inform us that the story we are telling is really inappropriate at a party, but we don't get any of these nonverbal signals online, only what people type. We are told that words comprise only 7 percent of what is being communicated. Thus, those who don't know how to handle the omission of 93 percent of all human signals (38 percent vocal tones and 55 percent body movement) either stay away or make dreadful mistakes. But can we blame them? As with a pilot trying to land every plane visually, sometimes it will work, but it can also end in disaster. We need more feedback.

Before Sending the First E-Mail

E-mail is a storm. People are buried under mountains of it. We like to joke at conferences sometimes by asking a crowd, "Who here wants more e-mail? Raise your hands!" Of course, no one in their right mind wants more e-mail. We all receive a ton of it. Now imagine you need something from someone.

If you've done your job well, getting a message into someone's busy inbox shouldn't be a problem. You've built relationships on the other side that will give you an edge over someone sending an e-mail cold. It also helps to understand when to send a message and when not to, particularly if you know that person is very busy and/or popular.

You'll have better luck if you heed the following:

- You have already made a connection with the person elsewhere (somewhere noncommittal, like Twitter), so the person recognizes your name. (For better luck, connect in two different places.)
- You have commented on the blog a few times, separating yourself from the crowd.
- You have taken part in a previous exchange where you'll have helped out that person first.
- You have been introduced by someone else (as mentioned earlier).

The most important thing about getting an answer to your e-mail is to have the person be familiar with you. Here are a few things you should consider:

- Have a topical, interesting subject line that catches the eye.
- Make it short.
- Finish your e-mail with the most pressing question; it will be the one thing you'll get an answer to.
- That's it! Expect an answer fairly shortly.

Transparency and Anonymity as Feedback

What happens on the Web that allows us to understand people? Well, first of all, there are two cultures that work together on the Web to amplify the signals we do get. One is a culture of transparency and, paradoxically, another is a strong respect for the sanctity of anonymity. Both work together to help us understand people better.

Anonymity has been a core element of the Web since its early days. Pseudonyms for Web users began long ago: If your first choice for a name was taken, you instead assumed any moniker you wanted, so we quickly became creative. In his book, *The Virtual Community*, Howard Rheingold talks about people he meets online with names like "poptart" and "Karlgirl." Pseudonyms, by definition, create anonymity, so people become more open about what they discuss; for example, problems about depression can be openly discussed in communities without fear of reprisal or rejection, and, on seeing the acceptance they receive, users open up even more. Anonymity can help people to open up, building confidence and leading to a greater sense of confidence about oneself over time.

Of course, many people use their real names online as well. While we both used nicknames in early BBS interactions in the 1990s, we began using our real names on the Web. This may not be for everyone; some use their pseudonyms forever, which is fine, too. It's possible that online transparency may have developed from the confidence that was created earlier in anonymity. In a culture of transparency, not only would we see other people discussing what was important to them, both successes and failures, but we'd also be able to see *who they are* by attaching faces and names to the experience. This is a vast improvement from communication offline, where we may see others and they see us, but know little about them at the end of the day.

This culture that favors anonymity and transparency as core values builds a sense of understanding, particularly when it happens over time and we understand the breadth of people's emotions. Not only that, but it also builds empathy, which we discuss next.

About Trolls

Anonymity changes the way people behave online. In the absence of social cues, studies have shown greater extremes in behavior than you would ever see in person. When someone acts in a way that the crowd doesn't approve of at a party, we see all other individuals react in both subtle and obvious way, from shifting their body away from the person they don't agree with to extreme verbal responses (i.e., "Shut the hell up"). We don't see the nonverbal cues online because they don't exist. We can't tell when people are annoyed unless they say so, and most often, they simply stop reading or paying attention, so the writer never gets the hint—and sometimes becomes even more extreme. This is called *trolling*, and it happens everywhere.

In order to act online, we need to develop a thicker skin, because we're effectively putting everyone in the same house, Big Brother–style, and hoping they get along. They won't. There will always be the people who want attention and refuse to be constructive, who even enjoy aggravating others, especially when there are no negative repercussions. Acting nice has a lot to do with what people will think of you later, and in circumstances where you can just walk away, you tend to care a lot less what people think or how they'll react. This behavior can be as antisocial as spamming.

Anyway, there will always be trolls on the Web. Ignore them; they love causing havoc and your appalled reactions will just egg them on. Participate instead where people seem to be at a certain level of discourse. Trust us, you'll sleep better.

Empathy as Feedback

While 93 percent of human signals may not be available on the Web, there is still much we can grasp from communication even when nonverbal cues are absent. We learn more because the culture of transparency causes the writer to discuss more about his or her thoughts and feelings than usual. But there's more to it than that. When people start to talk more about their feelings, we learn more about their inner complexities than may have been visible before. Being transparent on the Web fosters empathy, creating a stronger understanding of people's feelings both online and off.

Some of the first things we learn about people online are their feelings. Things that are unimportant tend not to be talked about, so instead we discuss things that we value, including a great variety of feelings. Learning these details encourages an under-standing of a person that is deeper than simply "my neighbor George," while also cutting through false perceptions of people, such as pretending they're fine or that they're tougher than they really are (though this happens online, too; see "About Trolls").

We develop important relationships with the individuals we encounter online because we learn more about them than what they show strangers at large. We see the real stuff that's normally hidden and that they don't necessarily have the courage to show everyone. And seeing this in a few people tends to build the feeling that *all people* have this depth, which offers a greater understanding of all humans we encounter, even though we may see little of their real selves.

Lurking versus Jumping In

In the online space, people often *lurk*. Quick definition: *Lurking* means not commenting, not showing any real digital footprint online, yet still consuming the information on a given site or network. Thus, if you're a representative from Apple and you visit all the Apple blogs looking for complaints, comments, threats, or whatever, but you never really participate in the conversation, you're lurking. It's not a negative term.

You might think we're going to recommend you jump in every time there's a conversation or post or tweet or Facebook status about your company. Not at all. There are perfectly good times to lurk. You can't engage in every conversation on the Web, and sometimes it might not be in your favor to join the conversation.

When should you jump in? When there's business value in the conversation. At some points, this may be a PR issue. Getting in and leaving a comment, even if it's something like "we hear you," is good for taking a little fire out of someone's belly.

You might reach out to a blogger to correct information in a blog post. When you do this, tread cautiously. It's really easy to find yourself in a pissing match with a blogger over a minor detail, and you may come off looking like the jerk.

Jumping in can also be great when it's unexpected. There's a story from November 2008 regarding basketball player Shaquille O'Neal and Twitter. Someone was using a fake account and pretending to be Shaq for entertainment purposes. (Twitter has lots of fake celebrities.) Shaq got wind of it and decided to jump in and be himself on Twitter. He got into the conversations right away, and immediately earned the respect of a community that appreciates the opportunity for two-way dialogue.

About Complaining

It's a natural human tendency to lash out at haters. After all, we feel hurt when we're being attacked, and we want to defend

(continued)

(continued)

ourselves. But you should just ignore the real haters out there. And there's a good reason for this.

There's a difference between real haters and those who complain about one of your products or the treatment they get from one of your employees. You should engage the latter. But when the anonymity of the Web combines with a straight-up bad attitude, the filtering ability of the Web's social tools is your friend. It's better to ignore some things than to argue back, because you cannot change people's minds about everything, and you can't be everyone's friend. You'll try your hardest to help, put in a lot of hours trying to make things right, but at some point, it just ain't worth it. Some people will never be happy.

If there's one piece of advice we can give you about how to deal with feedback, it's this: Praise those who deserve to be praised, and filter out those who are consistent complainers. This one rule will make the best use of your time, because it will bring forth the people who want to be involved, and it will let the haters shout up a storm in their corner of the Internet without it aggravating you too much.

The New Customer Service

If you're going to work as a trust agent, an element of what you do, every day, is customer service. You might not think of it that way, but your role is to empower and equip the people who choose to do business with you. Because you might not be used to thinking of yourself as a customer service representative, here are some points to consider:

- *Answer the phone.* On the Web, we're talking about this new "social phone," a term we learned about from Marcel Lebrun, entrepreneur and CEO of Radian6, a listening software platform. He looks at all these services (e.g., Facebook, LinkedIn, Twitter) as new phones that are ringing, asking for you or your company or your product, and when a company doesn't have a presence or listening ability, it can't hear the social phone ringing. The first step to taking advantage of the human powers of the Web is to be there to hear the call.

- *Learn the three A's.* Chris learned this during a (very) brief stint working at a restaurant. When a customer complains about something, follow the three A's: Acknowledge, Apologize, Act. This holds true for the Web. If you visit a blog and see a complaint about your company or product (or you), acknowledge it. Then apologize. Something simple: "I'm sorry it took you that long to get your file transfer problem sorted out." And act. Do something. Resolve the problem. One part of trust in being a trust agent is being reliable. Act as soon as you can so as to resolve the problem and to curb the anger escalation that happens when someone feels unheard.

- *Customers shoot back.* Realize that every customer can now blog, leave comments on Yelp.com and a hundred other sites, write reviews on Amazon.com, and complain on Twitter, Facebook, YouTube, and everywhere else that offers tools to communicate. Be ready for it, and be receptive to it. Sort out who's just complaining to complain versus who can be saved or converted. Learn how to adapt to an audience who has the same tools as the press to complain about you, and learn when and when not to engage.

Customer service is the new PR: From the 1950s until the early 2000s, customer service has been a cost center for any business. It has been a job where "get them off the phone fast" replaced "help them to remain our customer." Not good enough anymore. If you're in the game as a trust agent, this is an opportunity to do something more than a rival company. You can learn how to build relationships at a deep level using these online tools, which, in the interim, will crush your competitors and create great press for you.

The Three A's

Want a simple-yet-powerful recipe to improve your apologies? What? You didn't realize they needed improving? You need the three A's: *Acknowledge, Apologize, Act.*

- *Acknowledge.* Start any apology by telling the person that you accept that something happened. "I didn't meet my deadline."
- *Apologize.* Make sure you clearly and simply say that you're sorry, with *no excuses* tacked on. "I'm sorry, Ellie."
- *Act.* Explain what you'll do to improve or rectify the situation. "I've finished the work now and will better scope my time next time."

These simple steps, done in this order and sincerely, will make a world of difference as a trust agent.

Keeping Connected Across Distances

One of the simple ways the Web allows a trust agent to do business differently revolves around how others are using the Web. With people logging their status into Facebook, tweeting their goings-on on Twitter, and using all the new services that do things even more clearly and with layers of personal information, the Web has become an incredibly useful tool for extending relationships in the spaces between face-to-face conversations.

Imagine attending a conference you've traveled a great distance to get to. Several of the conference attendees are from the general surrounding area and know each other. You strike up some friendships and feel pretty happy about this. In the recent past, people would simply send e-mails back and forth, or make phone calls. But now you can look at your acquaintances' photos, status updates, and blog posts. The newer social software tools like Flickr, Twitter, Facebook, blogs, and other services allow us to have more robust senses of what's going on in someone's life while we're not in direct contact.

What if you needed to call a prospect to follow up on a potential sale you've been working on for weeks. In the old world, you'd pick up the phone or launch an e-mail and ask that person about the status of things. What you may not know, however, is that something fell through on the other side, or that the timing is off, or that you're about to send a some-what angry e-mail because you haven't heard from the person when the person has in fact been working on another very important deal.

Nowadays, there's some chance that your sales prospects are using these social tools and that you might have an opportunity to check in across the distance. Look at their status messages, their blogs, any of the places where they deposit online information about themselves. You may be able to determine whether this is the right time to try to close the sale. Maybe you should wait a day or two. Before, you'd have had to ask around, but now, it's on paper, it's out there, and you can just read it.

The Unanswered Email

You don't give blank stares to people who ask you questions, so why its digital equivalent? The unanswered email is un-comfortable; develop a habit of response instead. These tips apply just as easily to Facebook messages, instant messages over Skype, or any other medium, so learn them well.

- **Respond to everything, promptly.** Slow responses should be apologized for, and no response is the equivalent of a late meeting. No matter how small the response, send back *something*.
- **Everything is a test.** Your ability to respond and be intelligent in any communication medium is a representa-tion of your professional skills. Spelling, grammar, every-thing matters.
- **Don't Take Forever.** Your responses don't need to be perfectly crafted. Master the ability to let things go or your inbox will take over your life. Respond, send, gone, next.

Talking about the Weather

The relatively recent development of the social Web does something else. Increased connectivity through mobile phones and computers fosters a sense of community. Through things like status messages, seen most famously on Facebook, Twitter, and the like, we tend to not only see the profound but also the mundane. Seeing something as simple as "Having some wine at lunch, feeling sophisticated," may be trivial and interesting only to some, but messages such as these help build among followers a sense of *shared moments*. After all, haven't we all felt sophisticated while having wine at one time or another? Seeing other people sharing these feelings helps us relate to what a person is like, with both broad strokes and details filling out the sense that there is a *whole person* behind the keyboard.

How do you share these moments? You could write simple stuff one day and profound thoughts the next. If you're just a topical blogger, you may not reveal much of your personality and your life outside the Web, and that could be fine. But reveal little things, naturally, without making it a focal point, and people will develop a more complete view of you as a person and respect you more for it. Tara Hunt, author of *The Whuffie Factor*, calls this "throwing sheep," because it's fun and seemingly unproductive, but translates into a deeper sense of belonging. This translates to business, because people always think first of those they're familiar with (and those they like). It's natural to want to help people you enjoy spending time with, and hey, why not enjoy that time?

Maintaining a Human-Shaped Network

Human Artists know how to keep their "signals" live. Imagine that all these disparate conversations, these online chatters, these connections and human moves to network are like a telephone system: People's numbers change all the time. We lose touch. This happens even more in this loosely joined, "be one of the 150" world of ours, and because this network is vital to all the other things you'll do as a trust agent, it's important that you think about how to maintain the system.

- *Make constant touches.* Do what you can to keep a database of the last time you "pinged" someone with a small "touch." This means dropping a quick e-mail, a tweet, a

(continued)

(continued)

Facebook note, or whatever to say that you're thinking of someone or that you wanted to know how business was going. Wish everyone a very personalized happy birthday. Be as human as human can be.

- **Connect people together constantly.** If you have a friend who's really good at promoting music, keep your ears and eyes open for chances to slot that person into a relationship with others who can benefit. Connecting people puts you at the elbow of many transactions, and soon enough, people think of you as that hinge, that person who's key to getting things put together.
- **Link fervently.** On your blog, you've built a platform to reach out to people. Use it to point to the people who are doing good work. Raise the boats when you can, meaning praise and point out the up-and-comers if you sincerely think they're doing great work. They'll grow into larger roles at some point, and helping them early isn't a bad way to help both parties in a relationship.
- **Mix up the transmission methods.** When connecting with others, think about reaching out via different methods from time to time. Do you usually connect in e-mail? Send a Facebook video. Are you normally connected via Twitter? Ask if they want to connect via LinkedIn. This helps keep everything fresh. It's not vital, but it's a helpful tactic.

One-Way Intimacy

Trust agents reveal stuff about themselves both because they like to reach out to people on a human level and because it makes them more approachable: It makes friends and it helps business. But something that happens as a result of this kind of one-way intimacy can put trust agents somewhat at the mercy of the tribe that surrounds them.

What happens is that, over time, you reveal a great deal about yourself, but your readers don't reveal that much to you. On the Web, we live in a pull culture, where we grab the information we want, and trust agents have a lot of people asking for their attention, which means they can't always reciprocate. Thus, their audience comes to learn a lot about them, yet they know only a little about their audience.

There's a benefit to this that not many people pay attention to: The people who put themselves out there inevitably make mistakes in how much they reveal, and sometimes that means revealing too much. So, when all this information is out on paper, available through Google and so forth, there's a lot we can learn about our competitors.

The Web game becomes a series of decisions about what to put out online—and what not to. You should always be thinking not only about what impression you will leave today, but possibly what impression you'll leave in the future. Don't be one of those people who is fired because of a drunk Facebook photo! It's easy to think only about your friends when you're posting certain things, but remember, it's all on paper, and Google will have it forever.

How to Say No

Stephen Covey talked about the importance of saying no in his powerful work, *The 7 Habits of Highly Effective People*. Learning how to say no gracefully has become vital to our existence. As more and more opportunities come about, it becomes tempting to say yes to as many as we can. But saying no

(continued)

(continued)

gracefully means that you won't overbook, won't over-extend, and won't disappoint people who matter by saying yes so often that you're spread thin. Some tips:

- Start by thanking the person who asked you. "Thanks for thinking of me. I'm glad that I came to mind."
- Be very clear that you're refusing or saying no. "I can't take on this project at this time." Explain why.
- If you can offer an alternative, that's helpful. "My colleague, Justin, might have some cycles. Could I introduce you?"
- Be kind and gracious. You won't always be so busy. "I hope I'll be ready for you next time."

How Human Artists Sell on the Web

Nobody minds buying, but everybody hates being sold to. Although people sell on the Web all the time, they don't do it by selling. We've heard it described as "tell, not sell." Because they are personal, not mass media vehicles, web sites end up connecting very strongly to readers, and, as our friends, these readers expect a lot from us. We can't just walk around trying to sell them our product or service, because if we do, we'll look like awful people (oh, and also, it just doesn't work).

Thankfully, time is on our side. We've been known to take part in the "type and forget" style of blogging, but sometimes, crafting the perfect message can work in your favor.

By this we don't mean "craft the perfect press release." Press releases, while an important traditional business practice, are not as valuable as other sources of information. Don't focus on what the information (e.g., a blog post) says, but instead on what it *conveys* about its author.

Bringing ambient effects like this into the sales cycles is far more effective to long-term reputation and brand than pushing a hard sell. It is better to be there long before the sale and to share information that's helpful instead of information that's obviously a sell.

But you can't sit around forever waiting for a sale, and we know that, too. Look for gentle ways to convert information into sales on your primary social platform, and always in a friendly opt-in kind of way. Think, instead, about all this social interaction as "widest part of the funnel" sales activity, should you need to sell in one thing or another (and remember, we are *all* selling).

How to Ask for a Digg

It isn't easy to ask for something when you know it's purely self-serving, but sometimes it's necessary. However, in the case of Digg.com, when you get onto the Digg front page, it sends tons of attention and traffic to your site, which is a good thing. But it's self-serving. So when you need to ask for a favor, Digg-related or otherwise, you may feel kind of weird about it.

One way around this is to have an arrangement set up ahead of time. Instead of asking, "Hey, can you do this for me?" you can ask in advance if it is okay to ask for this kind of stuff. The "ask before the ask" makes us feel better when we need to make the real request. It helps your request be fulfilled, too, because the person has already agreed, so it's a win-win.

On a practical basis, this sometimes means setting up a separate group in your instant-messenger account (or e-mail) so that you know who's agreed and who hasn't. Sure, you can always choose to send outside of the list, but it's less likely to be agreed to, and, because it is self-serving, you'll feel a bit guilty about it. Better to have the list. It really works.

Getting Strangers to Trust Us

For a book titled *Trust Agents*, we really haven't walked directly into the land of "trust" and "how to" yet. Wonder why? The entire book is a recipe for it, but it's a slow roast, not a TV dinner. Let's give you some very direct and laid-out truths about what we know about trust and the Web.

First, trust on the Web is different than it is in person. You can have private communications online, sure, but we're talking mostly about public communication, the kind that happens on social networks, what we call one-to-many conversations (because it's one person talking to many others).

Second, the Web is about *channels*. Some are more like traditional media, and some are personal channels, but because that's the case, becoming a trust agent isn't just you being trusted personally, but becoming a trusted channel like, say, CNN. We want to be good people *and* good media. That's part of doing well online.

Social proof is far more powerful than you can imagine. If you see a headline that says "Gary Vaynerchuk Turns a Video Camera and Passion into $50 Million," you immediately want to know more about Vaynerchuk. Vaynerchuk is asked to keynote at conferences because people want to hear the answer to "how did you make millions by video blogging?" We want to hear about successes and popularity, but because of our limited time and attention span, we like to first hear that someone else thinks Vaynerchuk is great.

Second, "putting it on paper" means that every time you can show people how you've moved something forward, it gives you an extra level of reliability and trust. Each blog post that helps someone succeed, every time you share something that helps others, every time you open your personal network to connect two people who have business interests in common, is another opportunity to build others' confidence in you.

Simplest definition of trust: confidence and faith.

Be there before the sale. We trust Greg Cangialosi because we've seen him at conferences, at meetups, and online commenting on the same blogs that we read. Cangialosi is One of Us, and we know that he's there. Being there is every bit as important as anything else you can do.

Being helpful goes even further.

Some Real World Tips

It's all good to talk about proper communication on the Web, but what do you do in person? Watch yourself for the following bad habits:

- **Posture:** Stand naturally, as though you would when you weren't paying attention. Now look in the mirror. Bad posture is a sign of low confidence. Fix this one quickly through conscious straightening or therapy, like Alexander Technique.
- **Eye contact:** Are you making any eye contact, or are you making too much? Keep in mind that you'll act differently around people of a different social status.
- **Hovering:** Where you stand in relation to the people you speak to says volumes. If you're hovering, you can look needy. Pay attention to other people doing this and you'll see what we mean.
- **Smiling:** Confident people smile and show other signs of a good attitude, so smile with your *eyes*. People's reactions to you will change dramatically as you smile more.

One Simple Answer to Several Thousand Questions

When people ask Chris how he got to where he is in social media, his answer is always the same: Be helpful. Being helpful refers to many different things: It's a genuinely nice way to interact with people; it's a content creation strategy (people keep useful blog posts around longer); it's a guidepost to deciding what's worth doing; and, most often, it's the right thing to do.

Did Chris know it would also be the fastest way to rise above the fray of all the voices talking about social media? No. But it was one way to participate, and it's been helpful ever since.

Business in general exists to solve problems. If you're selling cars, you're helping with a transportation problem, but you're also in the education business. You educate buyers so that they can find a better fit in a car. You, one would hope, are being helpful.

On the Web, just as with putting it on paper, being helpful in full view of others helps guide you into being a trust agent, and that gives you the opportunity to do more business. And, unlike conspicuously making an effort to be nice because other people will see, the Web just displays it naturally, because everything is in public view. Being helpful becomes not only a great thing to do, but also a good strategic move.

The Association Test

We've all taken these kinds of tests:

Dog is to shark as cat is to...

(a) seaweed

(b) goldfish

(c) starfish

(d) spider

Sometimes you need to connect one thing to something else that's already familiar. It helps us to see something more clearly because it's *like* something else we already know. In that vein, here are things on the Web that we can make easy connections to:

Facebook is . . . about people, and it's about the fact that you can connect there without it necessarily being meaningful. We sometimes joke that it's easier to ask a girl at a bar to connect with you via Facebook than to ask for her phone number, because it's almost meaningless to connect there. Therefore, it's an easy place to make a first connection; it's unlikely someone will rebuke you for making a friend request.

Twitter is . . . like a huge conference call. It could be informational and helpful or just fun to spend time there. Either way, you learn who speaks to whom, find out what the general pecking order is, and discover more about individuals as you listen. It's a great tool for filling in the gaps.

Your blog is . . . your home base. Anything authoritative goes on here. If you had a shop, that would be your blog; you're trying to increase foot traffic and walk-ins as much as possible, so write often and make sure that what you write there represents you.

First Impressions

First impressions always last a long time, so leaving a good one is common sense. Doing it online, though, isn't as obvious. Your web site (or its outposts or Twitter, Facebook, etc.) can often be your first impression, which is why presentation matters.

This means your site should look professional. Everyone who sees it for the first time should be convinced that you know what you're doing on the Web and in real life. We don't recommend a blog that uses a template; instead, design custom stuff that better represents the business you're in.

It's strange how these kinds of signals convey trust or lack of trust, but we see it all the time. Domain names seem to give us a feeling about a person's presence on the Web. Don't believe us? Look at these domain names (we made them up as examples):

- http://mastertomorrowsradios.blogspot.com
- www.master-tomorrows-radios.info
- www.mastertomorrowsradios.com

Do any of these seem more authoritative, right from the start? Do you feel something more for one type of domain name than another? We think so, too. (Quick note: We have no problem with the folks at Blogger.com, who run the blogspot.com domains. It's just a point about perceptions. Good for you, Google. Please don't hate us.)

There are other signs of trust and impressions that we get from the Web:

- If you're using a social site, use a profile picture of yourself. No picture (usually some default ghost head) or a corporate logo sends a bad signal. We particularly like casual or arty pictures.
- When visitors see your name on another site, it reinforces that other authorities read your site, too. Aim for as many citations and links as possible so that people's first impressions will be "my friend likes this site, too."
- Testing shows that some logos improve people's chances of buying on a site by making them feel safer. It is the same with you and the mainstream press and other gatekeepers. If you've been mentioned by the *New York Times*, the BBC, or something similar, place the logo on your site. It's like wearing a suit to a business meeting.

Everyone *Seems* Like the Expert

Of course, there are plenty of opportunities online for misunderstanding. It's very easy for someone with a nice-looking blog and a good writing style to seem authoritative and yet to get all the information wrong; it's easy for us to think someone is bigger than they are. You probably know this already, but just to be sure: You can't always take everyone at their word, either in person or online.

Here's a quick tip for you: Always treat people as though they're regular folks. Your friends are fallible, after all, and you don't believe everything they say. You call them out when you don't agree with what they say (some of the time, anyway), and you hope they aren't sycophants, either. Treat folks like folks.

This is one of the big faults of those approaching people who are famous: If you approach them as though they're better than you, it won't work, because they can smell fear. (Just kidding, but nobody likes a toady.) People often approach Web celebrities this way, not wanting to take up too much of their time, but doing themselves a disservice in the process. We recommend that you try something else: Act like people are just regular dudes, never putting yourself into a situation where you might be seen as either loudly or fawningly trying to get their attention. (By the way, this works when you talk to attractive members of the opposite sex, too.) Here are some pointers:

- Look to create multiple small, nonthreatening encounters instead of one longer one.
- Don't ever approach someone when everyone else is around them asking for stuff.
- Ask someone else who knows them to introduce you instead of just coming up yourself.
- Don't ask for any favors.

- Just be friendly.
- Say things that are different than what people usually say to them.

All these things will differentiate you from everyone else and help people see you as different from the crowd of fans.

Reliability: The Big Secret

Years of working on the Web has taught us a lot, but one of the things you need to learn is the following: Reliability is a scarce resource. When people don't have a boss hovering over them, they tend to relax a little bit too much. Now becomes later, and later becomes late.

If you're paying attention, this means that reliability is one of the easiest ways to differentiate yourself. Be on time perpetually for your work, your meetings, and your emails. If you can't be on time, tell people early, not at the last minute. And whatever the case, offer constant updates as to your progress instead of long periods of (virtual) absence. You'll have already beaten out 75 percent of the competition.

Sharing versus Hoarding

Whether you're at the top of your game or just starting, you have to realize that you did not get there alone.

It's pretty common to feel that you are responsible for a lot of the success you've obtained, but that's not entirely true. There may be a few lone wolves out there, but most of us got where we are today through the help of many, many people. We didn't get there alone. The people who helped us didn't always need to; often, they helped because they saw potential in us or just because they're good people. We think you should be good people, too.

Which brings us to our point: Share your influence, even if you have only a little. When people want you to promote their ·thing, making a little effort (even if it's not blogging it yourself) can do tremendous good, because it shows a certain commitment to the relationship.

You may blog the idea, or you may not, but there are other options, too. Find a way to add to the promotion methods by suggesting something new, or use Twitter to spread the message in a more casual, "by the way" fashion. Whatever means you use, agree to help those who have fewer readers than you do.

How to Be Followed on Twitter

This is a tough one! Popular users receive a lot of "follow" e-mails every day, so it's one of the hardest things to do, but it's possible. In this section, adding the symbol @ before a name means sending a message directly to another user, like this: "@julien."

- Have a username that is similar to your name or a nickname you use elsewhere, so people recognize it.
- Have actual content on your page! Don't add people until you have several dozen messages sent through the service.
- Make sure you already have as many people as possible following you. We know this shouldn't matter, but it does, sorry. People like following important people.
- Never let your following/followed-by ratio reach more than 1 (i.e., follow less than 100 people if you're being followed by 101). This is a common rule of thumb people use to detect spammers.
- @ people often, and respond to other users' comments. Participation encourages inclusion.

(continued)

(continued)

- When you follow others, send them an @ message at the same time (e.g., @chrisbrogan or @julien when messaging us), so they'll see a message to them at the top of your page if they look at it.

From the Individual to the Group

There's a lot to learn about people, that's for sure. When we move from real life to online, we move from understanding relationships on a mostly individual level to an almost tribelike one, where we need to pay attention to the group and consider what it would like, too.

This is where things start to become different. We move from knowing very little about people online (essentially only what they choose to reveal) to knowing just enough about them that we can form a cohesive idea of what interests them *as a group*: what they embrace, what they reject, and what individuals in the community can come together for in a common purpose. That's what the next chapter is about.

7

Build an Army

You Can't Do It Alone

An individual can gain a lot of influence by acting alone, but doing so is missing half the picture. In addition to joining a group, *creating one* (and filling it with the smartest people you know) is the true path to influence online. If the social Web gives businesses the opportunity to rehumanize, it's at the risk of overwhelming those within a company entrusted with that role, because one person can't scale beyond certain limits. The answer is the subject of our sixth concept for trust agents: Build an Army.

When we think *army*, we think "Together, we can make a difference." The main job of an army is to have a huge impact, something that can't be done by one person or even a few really powerful ones. The goal can't be uniformly yours—or theirs. Both sides must want something out of it or it can't succeed.

Once you have established yourself as a trust agent, reaching the next level means building and dispersing armies around projects and opportunities rapidly and with a very loose command and control structure. Learn how to build an army, and not only will you master tomorrow's radios, you'll have strength in numbers and diversity.

A Quick Note about the "Army" Analogy

The United States was considered one of the world's top military powers through the 1990s. Up to that point, having the best armed forces meant having huge battleships, aircraft carriers, nuclear weapons, Bradley tanks, and other large vehicles.

At the turn of the century, the notion of what made an army effective was suddenly turned on its head. Effectiveness called for much smaller unit sizes, close-quarters combat methods, automated robotic troop augmentation, and several other shifts in the art of waging war. These changes had to be implemented almost overnight, but without these adaptations, the United States would be incapable of effectively engaging in warfare.

In many ways, this analogy ties in well to shifts in business communication. The Web has changed the game for all businesses. As inexpensive user-generated content is suddenly the best remembered of the Super Bowl ads, as blogs like those of Perez Hilton are outpacing mainstream publications like *People* magazine, and as smaller gestures are suddenly shifting perceptions, building your army of trust agents means understanding the new battlefield.

Your Generals: The Mastermind Group

One of the first discussions of mastermind groups was in Napoleon Hill's classic *Think and Grow Rich*. Since then, the concept of mastermind groups has become ubiquitous in the smartest of circles and in the best of strategy books.

On the Web, groups of highly motivated people within every circle have already joined together, helping each other reach higher ground, where battles can more easily be won. Sometimes they announce their presence. Other times, they're tucked away and just quietly doing their thing. Yet people everywhere are working together to improve themselves—to learn more and move forward. You may already be part of such a group, but if you aren't, you need to be looking for like-minded people to call your own.

Web-based interactions, which encourage this in ways that old-fashioned networking groups and learning groups can't match, are fluid, flexible, and connect people who aren't geographically aligned. What are the odds that the other great minds in your field live in the same town, or even within 20 minutes of you? But geographical location no longer matters when it comes to learning and building up each other's capabilities. With the new Web, mastermind groups can (and do!) exist in a digital-only form; in fact, they work better. This is because we align with others on the Web based on interest instead of geography, so finding people to connect with is easier.

When we started the Media Hacks[1] podcast, we realized that we could really be building a powerful group of people online, all highly connected to lots of people via their own blogs, podcasts, and other properties. We also had the ability to connect with all sorts of people who had their own skill sets. In effect, we were building a church (as discussed in Chapter 5, "Agent Zero") so that people could gather more often and build tighter relationships. And if we invite people into an episode of the podcast, we are inviting them into an exclusive, rewarding group where they

---

[1] www.mediahacks.org.

can benefit from our skill sets and we can benefit from theirs. Everybody wins.

This kind of exchange wouldn't happen if we all stayed in our little corners, doing our own thing. None of us, no matter how strong, would get very far alone, and we know it. So we form groups, join together, and develop mutual strategies to build something strong that we could never do alone. It's the *new* art of war.

An Army of Ronin and Why That Might Not Work

Anyone who's familiar with the work of acclaimed film director Akira Kurosawa knows the concept of the *ronin*, the masterless samurai who wandered the land during Japan's feudal period, usually after their master had died or had been dishonored.

There's a risk in the modern Web society: Many of us seem to want to be ronin. We used to need masters for protection, but we've had masters and we weren't sure we want one again. It's also easy to start your own business online. But will an all-ronin army work?

Businesses will be in a mode during the next few years where they don't necessarily want to hire many full-time employees, and this breeds more opportunities for solo practitioners of various skills. Attempting to marshal all these soloists into an army of trust agents may prove tricky.

The question is this: Can corporations trust external agents with their business relationships indefinitely? To extend that question, can trust agents develop deeper and scalable relationships with solo agents? Can you develop a network of trust with people who aren't really tied deeply to the same goal?

We can't answer this for you. It's a matter of learning how your organization might best work with trust agents and/or how you as a trust agent might go about structuring your business relationships.

There's a difference between the good nature that trust agents build with people of like interests and like-mindedness and trying to rally a group of hired guns. There are times for both, actually, but we prefer an army of excited friends and clients to an army of ronin. Commitment matters.

Two Social Contracts

General Motors is famous in social media circles for an early attempt at a social media contest that went awry, but you might be less aware of how GM "failed forward" into a really success-ful social media project after that failure.

- **The Failure.** For its Tahoe campaign, GM asked users to take a series of Tahoe clips, mix them into their own media, and then upload these to YouTube to be played on a special site. People did just that—except the videos they made were statements about Tahoe's impact on the environment (negative) and not really what GM expected.
- **The Success.** GM built GMNext.com and included a wiki and other user-editable areas where people could tell their stories of cars they were passionate about. People logged on in droves, gladly raving about their longtime passion for Corvettes, Camaros, or whatever car they'd owned.

See the difference? In the first case, GM asked people to advertise a new product. In the second case, GM asked people to share their passions, recognizing in the process that both sides would gain something from the exchange. In retrospect, it's obvious why the second effort succeeded and the first failed (food for thought while thinking about informal social contracts). Work with your armies instead of simply commanding them. They will be much happier.

The Power of Asynchronous Aggregation

The Web allows us to build power in aggregate as no tool has ever allowed us before. Instead of asking one person to make all the effort, we can ask 100 people for a fraction and get even greater results. We can ask people all over the world, and people can view things on their own time, allowing for a more powerful collection of capacity.

Imagine this task: Quickly build a useful encyclopedia of hyperlinked content. It shouldn't be possible without scores of project managers, tons of meetings, and mountains of coordination. Except—it was. Wikipedia has been around for years now, and it crushed an entire informational product category in offline publishing as well as in the online world, as well as making an encyclopedia a lot lighter to carry around. Amazingly, information gathered by random and often-anonymous amateurs trumped professionally turned-out encyclopedias. This surprised even Wikipedia's founders, who had started building a curated encyclopedia before Wikipedia.

That's a grand example, but several thousand smaller ones happen every day. People collaborate all the time via blogs, Facebook, services like Yelp, Twitter, and all over the Web, making large projects small and small projects incredibly easy. We're faster now. And we've all learned that if we can find more people to do a little part of the whole, we can move things forward in a very effective way.

It's important to realize that bringing people together may not always benefit your business. The power of crowds can sometimes build a powerful business, but it can just as easily destroy it, too. Wikipedia wiped out an entire group of successful businesses that preceded it. Wikipedia did this largely by accident, becoming a free business model that no longer needs ink, paper, or printing companies. That's the thing about armies: Sometimes, they work more effectively than you could ever have imagined. Build them, of course, but also watch out for others that may come along.

Mechanization: How the Web Works When You're Not There

In the mastermind group mentioned before, we have people who know how to work very powerfully with programmers to build huge automatic processes. We'd like to think of these as armies, too. One of the joys of the Web is that so much of it happens automatically: built once, but useful again and again. Instead of a librarian handing you the book you asked for, the programmers designed Wikipedia's engine so that you could find it even when all the lights are off at their office. Though there isn't yet any Rube Goldberg machine ready to make your favorite dinner, most of the important tasks we care to have done do have a machine ready to perform them. So, when we say "army," we don't just mean people. Your soldiers can also be machines.

Of course, machines can't do the jobs that people can (if they did, there wouldn't be much point to this book). But the machines fill in the spots *between* where the soldiers act. We may set up Google Alerts to search for our name in blog posts, but we have *people* tell us when there's a discussion going on somewhere that we may be interested in, because that's something a robot just couldn't figure out on its own.

The interesting thing is that, as technology develops (see our points about infrastructure in Chapter 4), the parts that can be executed by robots become more significant, replacing low-skillset human jobs, as in any other work environment. Our friend

Michael Boyle, for example, is building reputation management software at Exvisu[2] for large companies that are looking for a better way to keep an eye on what's going on online. That means his "robots" can attack the tasks of making sure that what people are saying online is cool with the companies he's dealing with, leaving humans to attack the tasks that are, well, human. It makes the army cheaper and leaves the humans more satisfied. (If you haven't done a menial job in a while, well, trust us.)

How the Web Helps Create Democracy

For the jobs that do still require humans, the social Web has facilitated even that. By requiring very little from each individual, the Web has made itself one of the most democratic tools for activism in history. Because we have access to so much right in front of us, we can help spread a message to thousands of people at once with only a click. We can donate a small amount of time or money and, with the help of a few thousand other people, dramatically impact politics or entertainment. We can make our views known more quickly, and with less effort, than ever before.

For these reasons and many more, a group of people on the Web is more powerful than a group of equal size anywhere else. It's true that 100 individuals in a city can pass out leaflets or ask their friends for help, but, by leveraging infrastructure, 100 Web visitors can have a message reach many more thousands. As their general, you can help.

Examples of this are everywhere now. We already mentioned Wikipedia, which has redefined research. Look at YouTube, which counts monthly views in the *billions* now, compared to any TV

---

[2] www.exvisu.com/.

network's monthly views. Hundreds of blogs outrank mainstream magazines and newspapers, in audience and engagement.

The power is in the fact that everyone has access, that everyone has distribution. In the old systems, distribution was the stumbling block. You couldn't just fire up your own radio station. Now you can turn on Blip.fm. You couldn't publish a book without a publishing house. Now there's Lulu.com or Blurb.com. For every gatekeeper, we've invented a new gatejumper via the Web.

Democracy, then, comes in the ability for all of us to produce and distribute our materials. We can all be stars, or at least microstars. In the same universe that has created Perez Hilton, you have the chance to succeed because you can circumvent the gatekeepers. People vote with their interest, with their attention, with their *trust*.

Oh, there's that word again.

The Ease of Spreading Information

It's easier to drive on concrete than in mud, and likewise, it's easier to spread a message when tools are there to help disseminate it. With the rise of social tools, spreading a meme has never been easier.

Consider an easy example: the simple e-mail hoax. E-mail counts as one of the main trustworthy ways for people to spread information (Forrester Research's recent surveys show that e-mail is the number one trusted information source online), so when people receive an e-mail from a person they know, they have confidence that it's true (because the trust they have in the sender is transferred). But factcheck.org is full of chain e-mails that, despite being false, are nonetheless popular even to this day.

But spreading information by e-mail isn't the only way. Now, blogs and recommendation tools like Digg and Reddit allow their communities to submit news and other ideas, helping them to be seen by tens of thousands of people. In effect, they are formalizing the information-spreading process, creating an infrastructure for it that minimizes the workload needed for people to receive information that's interesting to them.

StumbleUpon, another social recommendation service recently purchased by eBay, does it another way: by installing a toolbar instead of being a site in its own right, helping create a powerful, consistent traffic source entirely separate from web sites' usual dependence on Google.

This doesn't always work positively. In 2008, a CNN iReporter (the amateur arm of user-generated content for the U.S.-based news service) reported incorrectly that Apple's CEO Steve Jobs had suffered a heart attack.[3] The report knocked Apple stock from $105.27 to $95.41 in just a short moment, leaving everyone reeling.

Does this mean that citizen journalism, which spreads much faster than mainstream processes, is failing? No. This simply means that the system isn't flawless and that spreading incorrect ideas is just as powerful as spreading more accurate information.

Entire industries have developed around the idea of helping ideas become more sticky and spreadable, helping web sites develop content that allows them to be spread via these services. This is because recommendation engines use what you vote on to help determine what's relevant to other users, which in turn helps stories to be spread to the people who might be interested in them. Social recommendation has become so powerful that even *BusinessWeek* and other mainstream news sites now have Digg, Reddit, and Stumbleupon buttons on their articles. They know how much traffic and attention these sites can bring, and by

---

[3] http://machinist.salon.com/blog/2008/10/06/ireport/.

encouraging their readers to vote, each can help build toward the critical mass necessary to bring an article to its front page. Even traditional media like *Men's Health* magazine seem to be designing articles with the intention of reaching the front pages of these sites.

All this to say that the social Web is reaching prominence even in mainstream circles, and all of this is accomplished one vote at a time. Having an army of like-minded people whose voices are heard helps you reach the critical mass that will take your message to the next plateau.

Scale: The Importance of Café-Shaped Experiences

From the 1950s until the early 2000s, advertising and marketing followed along the path of the industrial revolution. Mass marketing followed mass production. Bigger supermarkets beat tiny markets. Chain restaurants replaced cafés. But the thing is, people's tastes seem to be changing. We don't enjoy the same beer anymore, an all-American Budweiser, like everyone else does. Instead, we like what the place down the street makes. It tastes better, it's local, and there's something cool about being able to talk to the guy who brewed it. And that does not just apply to beer, it applies to everything.

Report after report is coming out in favor of mass customization, the ability to "skin" products, to design them with us in mind. We want our own mark on everything. And with this desire for personalization in our product selection, our taste for mass communications is shifting back to a desire for more personal interactions.

Now that e-mail overload has crushed us, long after fax marketing came and went, with mainstream newspaper and magazine advertising in decline, and with television ads being deleted by digital video recorders, new methods are being tested all the time. Social media is one of these methods, and its intimacy is hitting a core group of people. They're sick of being pandered to, so they've stepped out of that line because the product at the end isn't interesting to them anymore. But it turns out they do love something else: the ability to connect with new people, share real experiences, and work toward a common goal, the same human interests that have meant a lot to us throughout human history.

We talked earlier about how the Web creates democracy, and it's important to think again about this as it relates to scale. The Web allows us to work within Dunbar's number. It means that we can build business relationships in different ways: Instead of just locally or in a specific vertical, we can channel and stripe and slice in many different ways.

It is *vital* to understand, though, that this medium has limits. There's a risk once you start thinking about mechanizing your online presence. Think of the difference between writing a personal message (in e-mail or on paper) and sending out an e-mail newsletter. The language changes. The personality changes. It shifts to what we're all trying to avoid.

To that end, think hard when planning. Think about this whole Build an Army concept with intention. This isn't about capturing the "most." It's the difference between passionate home-brewed beer aficionados and mass-produced mainstream beer. You're angling for the former, not the latter.

Some quick advice on this front: If you scale, be sure to keep these details in mind:

- Simple gestures matter. Saying a few words back to everyone you can touch in a given hour is a nice way for people to feel heard and seen.

- Remember to visit other people's sites, to participate in other people's things, and to make the conversation about them.
- Give as much as you can to your loyal community. Empower people within it to lead in their own ways. Promote people within your community to help them feel part of the core experience.

How to Bum-Rush the Charts

Wait, what does that even mean? To "bum-rush the charts" is a phrase that a few podcasters came up with in 2007 to describe the impact created by having a massive number of users simultaneously buy a song on iTunes: The resulting impact on the music charts was *huge*, but more importantly, it was great for the artist whose song was chosen.

So, how do you do it? Well, first, we'd like to point out that running an event like this that isn't aligned with the interests of your community is doomed to fail, not to mention that it's a little abusive. After Julien ran flash mobs (real-life e-mail-based mobs that would, for example, throw brief dance parties in subways), he was asked by companies to duplicate the process. Not only is it extremely difficult, but it's also taking advantage of people for the purpose of marketing—thus abusing a power you have for personal profit. We believe this would backfire on the organizers or companies involved.

That said, here's how to run a bum-rush-the-charts-type event.

1. Choose one thing you'd like to get your community to do.
2. Simplify the act as much as possible (make the link to the site obvious, blog about it on the day of the event, etc.). Reduce the act to the simplest process possible to combat short attention span.

(continued)

(*continued*)

3. Give the idea a cause. If it stands behind something a community cares about, it will be more successful. (We really hope you care about the cause, too.)
4. Reach cause-related influencers and help them spread it. If it's environmental, reach Treehugger.com. Note that online influencers are also guardians of their own communities, so a poorly planned project will fizzle.
5. Create incentive. What will happen if someone participates? There must be benefit for all involved.

Once you've taken steps in this direction, a compound effect can be created that builds great publicity for your project and helps people rally around what you do. Be careful with this method! If you fail, the apathy it creates will be a barrier the next time you want to get your army to act.

Bring Your Own Dial Tone: Small Powerful Networks

Jeff Pulver knows a thing or two about dial tone. A while back, he cofounded Vonage, the voice-over-IP telephone network that took on all the major telephone companies in the late 1990s. He continues to be a visionary, usually discovering key trends years before anyone else even knows there should be a trend there to discover. But we're going to give you one of his ideas now, and maybe you can bring it into your thoughts for the future.

In the old days, distribution was always the gate. You might be talented, but you weren't going to be on TV. You might be a decent writer, but there's only so much space in the newspaper, and even less in the book publishing world. The same was true with communication.

The U.S. government and other governments put the telecommunications industry under their watchful eye upon its creation, including regulation and also protection. Though this had some benefits and nurtured the growing communications networks, it also meant that competition was off the table. Voice over IP (VoIP) brought back an opportunity for competition by allowing people to use the Internet to complete voice conversations without the use of traditional dial tone and telecom company circuits.

Extrapolate this out to where social software has taken communications. With nothing more than Facebook, the average person can send text, audio, video, and other forms of messages between friends. Think about how this applies to mobile communications as well. The United States came later to the ubiquitous use of smart phones compared to the United Kingdom (let alone South Korea and the rest of eastern Asia), but that ground has quickly been recaptured by others.

Bringing your own dial tone is a powerful consideration when you think about building armies. It means that we now have the tools—and many of them—to communicate directly to empowered networks of passionate supporters. It's one of the reasons Barack Obama won the U.S. presidency in 2008: He had access to a mobile, active, wired constituency, whereas the opposing campaign worked almost entirely through landline phone campaigning.

This doesn't always mean creating your own social network, but rather, you'd do well to be able to use the various communications tools of the Web and understand how they reach your potential customers, your employees, your peers, and your champions.

When the Army Becomes a Mob: Kmart and Dad-o-Matic

This particular experience teaches the significance of trust, shifting dynamics, and how the Web (or at least the social Web) perceives the overt exchange of money.

Chris serves as an adviser to the company Izea, a company looking to marry advertising to the social Web. As part of his effort to understand the product, Chris wrote a sponsored post for his dads' blog, Dadomatic.com, on behalf of Kmart, one of Izea's clients. It was a cut-and-dried project: Take a $500 gift card, go shopping at Kmart, and then write about it—not necessarily favorably, just write about it. Period. In return, Chris would get $500, and one reader on Dadomatic.com would get a $500 gift card to re-create the experience for him- or herself.

The original post came out on December 2, 2008, and no one seemed to notice. Then, Forrester analyst Jeremiah Owyang mentioned it in Twitter and a storm ensued. The part of his tweet that apparently set off the storm was this:

" . . . Transparent? Yes. Authentic? Debatable. Sustainable?   No."

Suddenly, the denizens of Twitter turned angry, saying that Chris had damaged his credibility, that he was betraying his journalistic integrity, and that he'd sold out for only $500. Several conversations sprouted up, then blog posts. It blew into a full-fledged storm of posts, comments, and arguments on all sides almost at once, continuing for a period of more than 72 hours, day and night.

It became the topic of many debates: what people thought was right and wrong on the Web, what this meant for Chris, and what it meant about the social Web in general. The goal

(continued)

of this segment isn't to rehash the arguments. If Chris had it to do over again, he would have paid a bit more attention to people's sensitivity to how sponsored posts are perceived, and he would have started discussions ahead of the post to explain his stance prior to executing the project. Chris still believes in sponsored posts, however.

What is worth talking about—because it's what we learned most from—is how the crowd reacted.

First, reaction spread quickly. It brought up issues that a large group of people were obviously interested in. They had invested in Chris emotionally, so this experience was emotionally charged. It lasted a handful of days, but within those days, conversations were long, deep, multi-pronged, and intense. People worried about what sponsored blog posts meant to trust. They wondered whether this constituted a betrayal. They wondered a lot of things.

Another thing that may have upset people in this case was the overt exchange of money. This is worth dipping into. It's presumed that Chris makes a living from blogging. (He doesn't, exactly. He makes money because his blog showcases his abilities.) When an exchange of money—this sponsored post— was brought to the forefront instead of being kept discreetly offscreen, the transaction seemed to bring several questions and levels of uncertainty out at once.

All sponsored posts had always been disclosed before, but the dollar amounts involved had never been public. In Chris's readers' eyes, this somehow crossed the line between social and marketing norms. It reminded us of the fact that, although Barack Obama was a smoker throughout his campaign, after his election, and in the months leading up to his inauguration, imagery of this kind never made its way into the mainstream press. Even after more people knew about it, they didn't want

(continued)

(continued)

to see it. People didn't want to see Chris directly make money from his blog.

Years ago on television, married couples slept in twin beds. It was a requirement of television censors. We all knew that wasn't how married couples conducted themselves, but it was the desire of people at the time to keep things wholesome in this way. There's something similar at work regarding money and the Web. Certainly, many people make money online, and we know several ourselves, but there seems to be a strong divide between hoping someone is successful online and seeing an actual exchange of money.

But that isn't the only thing. The Kmart episode taught us a lot about how people behave on the Web and what they think of the people with whom they interact. In this case, we discovered that there are agreements, often implicit, between people and that these social contracts need to be clear and understood at all times.

The Social Contract

Any army worth its salt understands its job. The same is true of the general that leads them.

We don't often consider it, but we enter into contracts of all types all the time. Some are written down, but most are informal, the product of social signals that help us understand our place in any relationship. In the grand scheme of life, this ends up looking like a complex mating dance, incomprehensible to anyone outside of the ecosystem. But if we are going to Build an Army (or to be a part of one), we need to understand our place in its structure.

Of course, the armies of the Web may be more informal than their traditional counterparts. We don't march across miles of terrain, because our tools allow us to do it from the comfort of our own home, and we join groups more easily because the effort required is so much smaller. The goals are always a bit more tactical in these group efforts; the strategies usually feel mutually beneficial; the velocity at which we form and dissolve our units is dizzying; yet every one of these experiences requires some sort of social contract. Sometimes, companies do this successfully, and other times, not so much. It's important to know what you're getting into when you become part of a group.

Say you'd like something simple: You'd like your YouTube video to have a huge reach, with as many people as possible seeing it in the next 48 hours. A hundred views on a YouTube video won't do anything; it's only by giving it a momentum that you can make a difference. For that, you need an army. Each soldier doesn't need to do a lot, just view the video and spread it along, but the social contract between all of these people is simple: They're spreading an idea, whether it be for a cause or just for a laugh. Whatever it is, you need to be clear about the social contract you're forging.

With the YouTube video, the implicit agreement may be, "By passing this among your friends, you'll get the credit of finding something funny," the same way you can tell a joke in a bar and make people laugh. You also get credit for helping out, a small favor of sorts. For a cause, a person is feeling good by doing a little bit of good. If you're starting up something larger, understanding what each person is getting out of it helps, too, but it may be more complex. There needs to be a benefit for each member of your army. It's no longer just "duty" or "honor," but something else, and it's different every time. If you find it, you'll be one step closer to building your movement. But if you miss it, you may be in for some rough waters.

Give Your Ideas Handles

The real shift toward a win in building armies comes when the people you've chosen as your soldiers internalize your efforts, your ideas, your overall goals, and they take those ideas and make them their own. People in most cultures view themselves as the central hero of every story. We both do. Don't you? We love collaborating, and we're team players, but most people see themselves as the star in their life's story. With that in mind, your soldiers must be able to take your ideas as their own and develop their own uses for them.

Internal to an organization, this might come from setting up periodic meetings to discuss the shared vision of your Web efforts. You might share books and articles and blog posts that resonate with the group's plans. It might come from your internal blogs and the commentary that flows thereafter.

If you're a solo practitioner, or if you work in a blended environment of internal and external colleagues, sharing your ideas through blogs and video and other media is a great way to promote the ideas you're hoping to spread. Here are some thoughts on this:

- Write blog posts that equip others with the tools and strategies you're hoping to spread.
- Share liberally in online spaces like Google Reader, Delicious, and other social bookmarking and social news sites.
- Contribute to shared collaborative environments like Flickr and YouTube.
- Discuss and extend ideas on platforms like Twitter, FriendFeed, Facebook, or some of the newer ones.
- Write and distribute free e-books that equip others with your ideas so they can make them their own.

As a trust agent, there are many opportunities to collaborate and cooperate while competing. Sharing thoughts and ideas and equipping others to execute them might not seem, at first, to be good business sense. We feel differently. Most of the meat in business isn't in using these tools, but rather in *how* they are applied uniquely to your organization and your specific opportunities. The strategy your organization chooses will differ from those that other companies employ, and even if it's similar, the execution will be different.

In building armies, and giving your ideas handles such that people can execute in alignment with your shared beliefs, there's extra power that trust agents can use: scalability. It's our hope that your skills and experience will augment a great extended team and that your leadership through employing trust agent strategies will bring you better results. It has worked for us.

8

The Trust Agent

Art, Business, the Web, and Humans

Business, it feels, is becoming an art. Financial collapses across several industries hit the U.S. economy in 2008, and the entire world rolled into 2009 with even more troubles. Many organizations are still scrambling to keep afloat. On top of this, print journalism in the Western world is collapsing because advertising isn't supporting it anymore. Television and radio aren't exactly reporting record-making quarters, either. Companies need to evolve.

This is an amazing and unique time. Attention is scarce. The established leaders in many business segments have toppled or are on the ropes. The Internet has leveled the distribution playing field for media, merchandise, communication, location, and many other areas. It's at once scary and ideal, ideal because this is where trust agents excel.

237

The Web and new media give you the opportunity to reveal the human side of your business. Consumers can carry on conversations with brands like the Luxor Hotel and Casino in Las Vegas, Whole Foods, Home Depot, or even Hardees foods via the Web and its social networks. Not in the last 50 years or more has the balance of business interaction and communication been so in favor of smaller, more personal interactions than it is right now. Yes, some larger corporations continue to grind on and pay no attention to the little people, but that's not the norm.

Where will this all take us? We've shared with you six lessons to help you navigate this space. Do you *need* to be a trust agent to do business in the modern world? Of course not. Many people will do their jobs without thinking about any of this. Most of those jobs exist inside cubicles, with little in the way of entrepreneurial thought required and with a strong sense that someone else is steering the ship.

We think you're different. Maybe you've got the notion that you are capable of doing things better, that you have it in you to master these new radios. You may want to discover what others are doing to build trust and earn attention so you can apply it to your career.

As we wrap up the book with this final chapter, we want to discuss some stuff one last time and from some slightly different perspectives. The thing is, you can't for a moment think what you've read in the previous chapters is static information. This is a book, after all. By the time you're holding this in your hands, there already have been significant changes on the Web, and that's if you bought this book the first week it came out (and if you did, thank you very much, and we owe you a cookie).

So, once more, we bring you our thoughts on the trust agent.

How This Relates to Your Career

Being a trust agent requires a mix of strategies and skills that also serve other careers well. Thus, if you want to view what you've learned from this book in a different way, consider applying your new knowledge to your career at large. Obviously, much of what was discussed deals heavily with online presence and how businesses can rehumanize themselves on the Web, but the skills discussed in this book are quite readily adaptable to other pursuits. Think about it.

- *Make Your Own Game*. Learning how to build market advantage will serve you in every business venture you're involved with, be it an older business seeking to revitalize or a startup looking to take the world by storm. By making your own game and forcing your competitors to keep up, you leave them at a disadvantage at every turn.
- *One of Us*. Being seen as connected with others is very useful in any people-facing job, be it on the Web or off. The best restaurant servers practice being One of Us, as do the best professional entertainers, people in real estate, and more. To be accepted at your new workplace, act like you're already accepted, like you're already One of Us. Soon enough, you will be.
- *Archimedes Effect*. Understanding leverage helps with everything from mastering your personal finances to understanding how to negotiate for a better job. Leverage means never again having to reinvent the wheel; it never goes out of style.
- *Agent Zero*. Connecting to others and building small, powerful networks is useful in every kind of role, including fundraising for schools, building community groups, or forming a very powerful agency with multiple offices on several continents. This trait also will help you with your new job search needs,

forever. Have a wide network and you'll never be in need of work.

- *Human Artist.* People skills are essential. Learning the etiquette of circumstances, understanding how to interact with people, and mastering all the other traits of being a human artist play nicely into the experiences you will need over the course of your career. The best public accountants, the most successful doctors, the leading teachers are all the best possible human artists. Etiquette and human understanding are the cornerstones of any meaningful life.

- *Build Armies.* Leaders aren't simply those who are the best at doing their jobs; they are the best at helping others to grow and gathering those people's skills to their command when necessary. Operations experts, executives, and a whole host of jobs lean heavily on the ability to train, scale, and lead a group of talented individuals, so building these skills is an amazing career move. Not only that, but the more people you have vouching for you, the wider your reputation spreads. That's a lot better than telling people about yourself!

Though this book was written as a business book about using the Web, the skills of a trust agent can be applied to many endeavors. If you think about it, this is another chance to make your own game. Perhaps you'll learn how to adapt your trust agent skills to other roles offline and have similar success. If so, we'd love to hear about it. Email stories@trustagent.com to tell us how you make out.

Master Tomorrow's Radios

What happens now? You now know a little about the current state of affairs, but what's going to happen in the future, and how can you prepare yourself now?

As we said, much of what you read here is not just useful in online interactions. That's because how trust works isn't a new thing. What's changed is that trust flows in different ways because of a new communication medium; similar shifts were seen in the past with the advent of radio, television, and, yes, even smoke signals.

You can think of the Web and its evolution as the next radio. You could even differentiate between the first web of the late 1990s and the newer web of the 2000s. This newer web is to the old web what TV was to radio in the 1950s. Your goal as a trust agent is to master tomorrow's radios before others, and thus, make your own game.

This requires perpetual lab work. Technological advancements won't stop. Even this book, published in 2009, would be obsolete if we focused on the tools of the day only. Instead, we gave you a framework to consider, and we spoke from the perspective of the day's tools. However, the steps you must take to stay in the game (your own game) require you to keep innovating and to move from the tools of the day to the new generations of tools that come along.

Keep this premise in mind: As everyone understands how to make TV shows and magazine articles, and as the establishment learns how to better market and advertise within those media, your goal is to be the best communicator the Web has ever seen. As more people flood into the Web and learn what you know now, your goal is to find that next radio, the next channel, and to master it the way you did the current online space using what you've learned here.

The difference is that the guiding points throughout the book extend beyond the Internet. We didn't write that you should Make Your Own Facebook Game. We don't think the game is on Facebook or Twitter or whatever social network you are on as you read this book. Making your own game transcends the Web as we know it right now. What's more, it's a principle that will serve you well elsewhere.

Keep your eyes on tomorrow's radios.

How Frames and Perspective Matter

Have you ever heard of the term "abundance mentality"? It's a phrase coined by Dr. Stephen R. Covey in his powerful book *The 7 Habits of Highly Effective People*. Essentially, Dr. Covey recommends that we adjust the lens through which we see the world so that we see everything around us as abundant. Thus, if your coworker gets the promotion ahead of you, rejoice. There are other promotions to be had. In this mind-set, you don't think about competitors. You just work hard at what you're doing. It's a frame, and if you think from that frame, the actions you take will be different than if you think the world is out to get you, that you're the only one deserving of a promotion, and that your competitors are all evil scum.

Understanding your own perspectives, and the way they frame what you do, how you think, and even what you can envision, is a powerful ability to cultivate. For example, if you see Facebook as a place to reconnect with old schoolmates, that's one perspective. Thus, you'd frame all your activities there around leisure and social interactions of the nonbusiness kind.

However, if you see Facebook as a vast store of demographic data, where your customers, competitors, and prospects all freely give away their personal information, you might think of ways to capture that information, analyze it, and do something more with it for your business purposes. You might develop a simple application that several thousand people try out, and with each acceptance, you would receive much more data to review and act upon.

As you think about the skills one might need to be a trust agent, you must analyze things with a particular strategy and end result in mind. As such, you may think about things like the difference between doing someone a service in public versus those good deeds we do privately. Sometimes, it's important that others know you're doing a favor or a kindness. Other times, you don't want to draw attention to it. Moments like that relate to how you perceive things and to how you frame your actions based on those perceptions.

A Few Frames to Consider Adopting

As a trust agent, think about some of these frames when considering your work. These are based on the six lessons taught throughout the book and are a great way to advance your business and build better online relationships.

- How can I connect other people? If you're at the elbow of every deal, using your Agent Zero mind-set, think often about ways you can connect people of value. Sometimes you can do this simply, like mentioning out loud (like on a blog) how Ed is a good person to know. Other times, you can be purposeful and connect people who've lost a job to prospective employers. Both benefit, and you make your ties stronger.
- Where's the leverage point? When thinking about making moves, like buying a new domain, changing jobs, writing a book, or whatever, ask yourself what the move gets you. We both consider this book an opportunity to speak with people outside our existing circle. It's a way to leverage our experience into new places.

(continued)

(*continued*)

- Is he One of Us? When evaluating new products or services, ask whether the company has a presence in the space the product belongs in. For instance, would you sooner buy video games made by lifetime gamers who keep a blog and who talk to their community or from an opaque shop where the web site only shows you how to buy more things? Find ways to help those inside your community.

- Is there a new game here? This is a powerful frame for entrepreneurial types. Trust agents who work on the Web have to perpetually keep their eyes open for new potential business opportunities. Attention is a powerful thing to have, and games often draw attention. As such, they are worthy of a trust agent's consideration. Where's the new game? Are there rules you could ignore?

Those are just a few to consider. You might develop new frames all your own as you keep your perspective tuned and adaptable.

"Yes, and . . ." and How That Applies to a Trust Agent

One of the basic concepts behind improvisational comedy provides an example of how you, as a trust agent, should think. This is the practice of saying, "Yes, and . . ." Here's how it works: No matter what the situation, in improv the intention is always "yes, and." The premise of this rule is that to collaborate, you can never crush a scene by saying no to the imagination of another participant. Thus, if two people are in a scene, and one advances the story in some way, it's important to answer any question by first displaying your acceptance and then advancing the story: "Yes, and . . . ."

For instance, if Chris is on a stage pretending to read a newspaper, Julien might say, "Did you read that the circus left town in a hurry?" Chris might answer, "Yes, and they all got into one tiny car to do it." He's not just reacting or agreeing with him; he's also adding to the story.

"Yes, and" is important because it helps contribute to any scene in which improvisers are involved. So when you're on stage, it's always more important to accept what someone else just said (that's the "Yes") and then add to what they're contributing (that's the "and").

The premise, as it applies to doing business on the Web, is this: Be open to the possibility. One secret of trust agents, and how we formulate our ideas around making our own game, building armies, thinking about leverage, and other forces at play, is that we think with a "Yes, and . . ." mentality. The opposite is to be close-minded, to look at what could go wrong, to consider the negatives. This one tiny detail makes a world of difference in how one perceives his or her options on the Web.

To that point, practice saying "Yes, and . . ." to everything, if only in your head. Imagine sitting in a meeting with your team when the VP of marketing says, "We're really losing traffic to the site. Maybe there's just nothing more we can do to attract attention." That's a fairly negative view. But what if you append a "Yes, and . . ." mind-set to the statement.

"We're really losing traffic to the site. Is there anything else we can do to attract attention?" "Yes, and one way is to rebuild the level of engagement and try to answer in a more human fashion." Immediately you've added something, and you're on the solution side of the equation.

Understanding improvisational comedy has made an actual business difference in our lives. One great book on the subject is *Improv Wisdom*, by Patricia Ryan Madson. The lessons put forth in that book might very well help you understand how improv applies to being a trust agent, and how that might help with your business.

How to Make Friends (and Why It Matters)

Around the time this book was published, Julien had turned 30 and (this may make you laugh) was starting to feel old. He noticed a long time ago that as people get older their social circles tend to get smaller, including closer and closer friends until, at some point, they find themselves hanging out with, say, just one other couple week in, week out. He was bothered by this; after all, no one wants to know fewer and fewer people and lose touch with others. It's just something that happens.

So Julien started to find ways to go out more. He went to more events to meet people and generally put himself out there more. He realized he needed to do this to keep meeting new and exciting people, especially those who were doing exciting things, thinking about exciting stuff, and just generally making things happen.

Afterward, he determined that there was a trick to this. He couldn't just go out there with the hope of meeting people; he had to create value for them. In effect, it became evident that people need to give something of value to help create relationships, even if that something is small. It can be a smile, telling a joke, or letting someone in front of you in the checkout aisle. Little things actually worked well. It's like a tiny gift, but one that started an exchange. And it's a lot like participation in the social web; in fact, it's almost exactly the same, since the social web is just one more place to interact.

So if you were to retain one piece of information, one tip, about the social side of trust, it should be this: You need to be liked, and you start becoming likable by *being worthy of being liked.* Be kind. Be patient. Be humble, on time, and generous. Be that person you would like to be friends with. Likability and the related trait, intimacy, is one of the biggest factors in trust, and it's also one of the easiest to develop with people online. So work on that first with people, before you try to create transactions or take things further. It makes a world of difference.

Start Small

There is a well-known online article titled "Filthy Linking Rich," by Mike Grehan,[1] that is highly read and referenced in web entrepreneur and marketing circles. It states, very simply, that those websites with a tendency to gather a large amount of attention and, as a result, a lot of web links from other sites will have a tendency to get even more links in the future. People were generally aware of this basic concept in other ways; everyone knows the phrase "the rich get richer," for example. Most, however, don't know why. What we do know is that in any circumstance where there are some people with resources and others with very few, those with more will get a bigger cut of any future resources. Mike Grehan noted in his article that, for whatever reason, this seems to apply in a lot of places, not just with what's in your bank account.

This is the result of a power law, often referred to in business as the Pareto Principle or, colloquially, the 80/20 rule. An examination of this law resulted in some pretty popular books, among which are *The Long Tail*, by Chris Anderson, and *The 4-Hour*

---

[1] www.keyworddriven.com/filthy-linking-rich-and-getting-richer.html.

Workweek, by Tim Ferriss. The way a power law works is that, unlike a bell curve, most of the success comes to the very few. They have more advantages than the rest, so they get more of whatever is coming up. So a power law is a representation of what comes to mind when we say things like "the rich get richer."

When you think about it, there really is a winner-takes-all truth to almost all situations where there is competition for a limited resource, whether it is for share of a particular business niche or for attention. Those with larger access get more access, those with less continue to get less.

If it is profitable for you to be the first person to come to mind when people think about widgets (or whatever business you're in), having an understanding of why will help you rise in prominence and fast, because then you will be more likely to get even higher. In other words, it's easier to get up to the top of the curve if you're already on the way up. We know it should be obvious, but sometimes it isn't.

So if you're looking for a lot of attention from a lot of people, start by having one small success that gets you *some*, maybe even in one small community. After you find that one success, let it propel you toward others. Keep working until you have that first victory, and then use it to leverage yourself into the next one. After that, the key is to maintain your momentum.

As Mike Grehan stated in his article, "Getting a million dollars from one person is hard. However, getting one dollar from a million people is really not so difficult." Taking small steps: that is what will help you reach your goal.

The One Difference

There really are two ways to get to the top of the pile: push other people down or raise yourself up. We've gotten where we are by being constructive and collaborative, working positively with others, and trying to be the better man. We bet you can too.

When trust agents compete in these winner-take-all industries it is done quite differently than in traditional business. Old business might try some pretty harsh tactics, but we live in an era where there are no secrets, so you should behave accordingly and consider carefully how you'd like to be known or talked about.

Julien is very fond of a saying Chris has on his blog: "You guys can try your tactics or do whatever you'd like. While you're doing that, I'll be over here improving my business." That means, I'm taking the high road; I'm not trying to bring anyone else down. Instead, I'm trying to raise the level of what I'm doing, so you have to compete *with me*, not the other way around. And this strategy works.

Be Wary of Praise and Awards

The Internet has a weird penchant for praise, and awards, and lists. It seems there's always a new list of the best bloggers, the top real estate professionals, or the very best marketers of the year. There are little popularity contests, explicit or otherwise, that can accidentally attract your attention and distract you from your goal.

Sometimes the praise comes from statistics. Marketers have spent an entire decade talking about pageviews as an important measurement of their online efforts. Think about that for a moment. Imagine that your web presence is a store and that those pageviews are potential customers. Does it matter how many people are walking around your store if they are not buying anything? Of course not.

Attention is great, but if it's only attention, then it's not sales. And let's not think of sales as just money, either. If we replace "sales" with "the action I want you to take next," then that's the real measure of success. Is there any other?

Now, think about praise. Does it matter if your web site is one of the Top 100 in the world? Yes, there's some social proof to being in that category, but that's nothing if you have no follow-through. When Chris's blog reached the Technorati Top 100, balloons didn't fall down from the ceiling. No one knocked on the door with a check. He didn't get a pony. He just went on and continued to work.

If you focus on the awards and the praise, you're missing the real value of the attention. Now, don't let us tell you what to value. You might be building your online presence to do business. That's great. You might simply need a platform to build your personal brand. Excellent. Maybe you're helping nonprofits with all the ways a trust agent can benefit that space. Perfect.

Worrying about star ratings in YouTube and reaching Delicious.com/popular and other online measures of temporary value is going to distract you from the actual work you're trying to accomplish.

Let's talk about making some new games, for instance.

Six Games You Could Have Made and Still Can

In the spirit of making your own game, here are just six strategies used by people mentioned throughout the book that you could use to increase your web presence:

1. *Write a content marketing blog about a passion of yours.* Gary Vaynerchuk sold more than $50 million in wine and spirits based on his passionate Internet video show, Wine Library TV. He crushed the category when there were plenty of wine critics and other sources of information out there. Gary made

his own game, and now the world is chasing him. Why not build a blog or videoblog around something you're passionate about that links to a product or service? Maybe you're passionate about fashion. There are several programs that could tie to what you're passionate about and create content around it.

2. *Build a small, powerful network.* Bryan Elliott assembled marketing and advertising professionals located in Orange County, California (the group has since spread out a bit into the rest of the state). They work in and among themselves to source new projects. They stay abreast of each other's job changes. They help each other develop and grow. You can build a small, powerful network and be Agent Zero at the core of an important group related to your industry.

3. *Become the name brand of a specialty.* Christopher S. Penn created the Financial Aid Podcast because he felt it was a great way to communicate with students and parents of students looking for general financial advice and specific information about student loans, his particular line of business. By being One of Us, Chris has delivered hundreds and hundreds of helpful podcasts (swing by http://www .financialaidpodcast.com and listen to one), and as a result he has made his company millions of dollars servicing student loans. Before we told you about Chris, who could you name in the student loan game? No one. Can you become the name brand of your field by mastering a new medium? You bet.

4. *Master leverage and use it for good.* Beth Kanter is our patron saint of nonprofits and technology. She helps various causes understand how to use the Web's new tools to raise money and improve the quality of their efforts. In so doing, Beth takes advantage of the Archimedes Effect. She understands

how to find opportunity and tap into it for the greater good. Can you find leverage points to facilitate your work and create value?

5. *Sell by generating human trust.* Aaron Wall of SEObook.com is able to sell valuable information online not only by offering exceptional quality, but also because he mastered being a human artist. He learned that trust came from constant exposure to his work, such that people began to accept him as the default in certain categories (search engine optimization and marketing). As people saw more and more of Aaron's work and as he was cited in more places as the SEO expert, that level of trust gained from exposure made his products the first mover in the spaces where he intended to sell. Are you building enough awareness and exposure to be the default in your space?

6. *Make an army to power your change.* Frank Eliason from Comcast changed the way we think of customer service in the Web-facing world. But as he is only one man, Frank needed an army, so he trained more people to handle the same job. Building up groups of people to work on projects for you should be a priority. Never hoard your expertise or your angle. Instead, find ways that you can work with others to be successful. Can you find a way to empower armies of helpful people to make your projects expand even more?

If You Were to Write the Next Chapter

One important point of being a trust agent involves understanding that no one person has the full answer any longer. If you haven't absorbed that idea fully since Surowiecki's *The Wisdom of Crowds* or since Friedman explained value chain disaggregation in *The World is Flat*, then think about it here once more.

You are wiring the Web. Your links in blog posts tell Google where to find the good stuff. Your contributions to Flickr, YouTube, Delicious, Twitter, Facebook, Wikipedia, Craigslist, and countless other sites are why the Web exists, and without you there is no reason to visit any of those places.

As the Web has evolved, several previously existing business models have been toppled. Getty Images was seriously destabilized by the coming of iStockPhoto.com (until they bought them), not to mention Flickr. Crowdspring.com and several other sites exist where people are rapidly solving each other's design problems for very little money and with almost no friction. For all that we both know about the Web, and for our combined years of experience, there's someone out there, probably 13 years old, who has several key strategies figured out that we haven't even thought about.

Trust is the most significant factor at the source of all of that, and understanding how businesses can rehumanize the Web is really only one lens. There could be another dozen books written about trust, people, and the Web, and they wouldn't cover it all. For all we know, that's *your* next book to write.

So along with everything else we've written, think about that. Part of what you do as a trust agent is realizing that everyone else has great ideas, that they are professionals, and that they have angles you've yet to consider. Can you hand over the keys easily?

How You Can Help

In trying times, people need all the help they can get. And as time goes on, people increasingly will be looking to the Web to help them. That's where you come in.

If you've been following our advice, by this point in your reading you should be thinking about being One of Us somewhere in a certain community, either online or off. But you may not know what to offer them. Our suggestion is that you offer them the tips in this book or the book itself. Here's why.

As much as possible, everything you've just read has come from experience, and we've tried to cut the fluff, leaving you with tips that you can use with people, on the Web or otherwise, to help you build trust *today*. But you aren't alone in needing more concrete information and advice. Plenty of others do too, maybe even more critically than you. And here's the thing: By offering them concrete help in their time of need, you're doing exactly what a trust agent would do—offering genuine, authentic assistance. People will see that and respond to it by opening up, by letting you in a bit more.

It's in this way that helping others is probably one of the most effective ways to help yourself. By spreading ideas that help others, you get credit and people get the help they need. It's win-win. What a change from the scarcity mentality most people live with every day, isn't it? And that's one of the best things about the social web; people are deeply interested in sharing with each other. If you're like us, that's pretty different from the rest of your usual life, where people cut each other off in traffic and argue over parking spots, and that's just why we like it. We have a feeling you'll enjoy it too.

Three More Things You Can Do to Add Value

As a trust agent, your work might be mostly in the space around business development or as some kind of customer advocate plus. Or, you might just use these strategies for your own ends inside or outside of a company. No matter where you want to apply the ideas in this book, here are some ways in which you can add value:

- *Feed the machine.* The Web revolves around human contributions. Location-based platforms like BrightKite seek to be fed information and pictures. Flickr wants to know where the picture of the bright yellow coffee shop was taken, down to a pushpin on a map. Amazon really does want to know what you thought of the *Fight Club* 20th Anniversary DVD. There are many ways to contribute. Find a few that aren't too painful and do it. For instance, Brian Solis, a successful PR practitioner, has taken tens of thousands of photos of Internet personalities and provided his professional-quality work on Flickr to be used under Creative Commons licensing. In this very simple way, Brian has created a simple, searchable database of who's who in the Internet space that you can use before attending any conference.
- *Be helpful.* Just for the sake of doing it, be helpful. It's the act that keeps on giving. Since so many people are in it for them, this one idea is worth more than you'd imagine. Doing very simple things without the emphasis on any kind of quid pro quo makes it much more meaningful, and the ways you can do this are endless. Help others with a job search. Donate your time to causes that can't otherwise afford you. Create five times as much free value as you do for the parts where you charge. Whatever the method, be helpful.
- *Make things.* It's okay to talk about things and report on new developments, but try and make things that others can use. You might not be a software developer, designer, or many other things, but you are figuring things out, and you probably have some information others can use. Take the extra time to create the occasional e-book—not as a sales tool for your

stuff, but because it's nice to help and because you're contributing to the larger body of work.

These three ideas all run along the same theme. It's important to add value to this space while being a trust agent. Call it your own version of stewardship.

Ways People May Trash the Lessons in This Book

1) "Big businesses won't adopt any of this."

That's entirely possible. Or, what might happen is that big business will take the concepts and run with them in its own way. The original Voice over IP revolution was expected to be a situation where VoIP would topple all the major telecommunications companies. Instead, the telcos rolled over and absorbed VoIP into their DNA without stopping even to belch.

Besides, it's not as if the things big business won't do aren't profitable. Often, the companies just aren't agile enough. And if big businesses never adopt it, that's fine. Small businesses would love a piece of the action that big business won't touch. This is something bootstrappers should be happy about.

2) "Things aren't that simple."

There will certainly be a few people who read this book and think, "It can't be that simple. Six things? A formula? Life doesn't work that way." If that is your argument, dear sir or madam, we're afraid we'll have to agree with you; of course it isn't simple.

The reason we decided to go with the format we did is that it's easier to look at and say, "Yep, we're doing that," and "Yes, we're doing a bit of that." At the same time, you can quickly look at something and say, "Oops, here's something we haven't tried." Simplicity will help you remember, so don't fret about it being uncomplicated.

3) "This isn't very measurable."

Yeah, no kidding. Neither is networking. Radio wasn't very measurable when it started. TV wasn't very measurable; in fact, it still isn't. In all those cases, the numbers collected on them today are still more of a formula than a true number. While we certainly look for direct numbers to measure, such as investment versus yield, reduction in advertising spent, increase in conversions, and so on, we won't dispute that some of this is more experimental in nature. But if you consider that you're first to the game, do you really expect there to be a roadmap with no risks? That's another book, a five-year-old book in its fourth edition.

4) "This sounds very amateurish."

We're willing to say that every innovation in the world started with a chorus of people telling the innovators that their effort was amateurish in comparison to the tried-and-true ways. We know two Steves who started making PCs in a garage in Silicon Valley who were told their computer wasn't all that interesting when compared to the current status quo mainframes. You can keep doing what you've been doing if it's working for you, but we're going to bet you have a sense that we're onto something, even if it's something small.

5) "This takes too much time."

So does planting your own food, but if you dare to compare the taste of the vegetables you grow in your own yard versus what you buy at a grocery store, you'll wonder why you paid for colored cardboard all this time. Being a trust agent is a bit artisan in nature. You can do sales or PR or marketing or other business communications work without doing what we talked about, but will it taste as good? Will you be able to sell it for as much as we sell our organic stuff (a $20 billion industry, by the way)? There's a whole section of society that's now refusing to buy your mass-produced, one-size-fits-all offerings.

Where We're Going in the Next Few Years

This book was first published in 2009. At this point, the Web sites people pay the most attention to (besides search engines) are YouTube, Facebook, MySpace, and primarily the social networks. They've surpassed porn as the types of sites people spend the most time using on the Internet (we know, we were shocked, too). Twitter is striking into mainstream press, and people are joining and leaving more social networks than ever before.

Advertising spending offline is on the decline. Spending online is risky. Companies like Federated Media and others are working to shift how people interact with what will be left of advertising, and it won't be banners. Media makers like bloggers and other content-minded people are launching more blogs than ever. The 2008 Technorati State of the Blogosphere reported more than 900,000 blog entries are posted every day (see Figure 8.1).

What does all this mean for trust agents? What does it mean for you?

Attention is and will continue to be our scarcest resource. As such, in business, we feel that trust and the humanizing of business is where the action is. Advertising as it was from the 1950s to 2000 will continue to decline, and in its place, we'll see more activities that drive a closer, more unscripted relationship

Figure 8.1 Technorati State of the Blogosphere, 2008

Source: http://technorati.com/blogging/state-of-the-blogosphere/.

between companies and their target audience. In B2B, this will take the form of informative media and deeper social network interactions. In the consumer space, this will become something more of a mix of user-generated content, blogger relations campaigns, affiliate marketing, and similar less-protected marketing communications blends.

Public relations, if one defines it as a role to try and get ink in the *Wall Street Journal*, becomes more of a listening, reputation, and communications management position, with far more interactions falling into blogger relations, brand facilitation, and situations where a company's story and language need stewardship. With communications channels becoming narrower and much more numerous, it becomes less about control and more about being part of a dialogue with a number of active community leaders.

Brands will need to earn a place in our heads with a sense of personal intimacy, as well as the consistent messaging they've been using to get them to trust us. Sometimes, this may include a sense of vulnerability that will help us see the human beings behind the corporations; this may even involve admitting they were wrong. Losing control like this won't be easy, but those who make the transition will see enormous benefit among the people who talk about them.

All this humanizing is normal; in fact, the only reason we think that it's crazy is because most of us were born in the brief period where mass media was the only game in town. But remember, that's only been the case for a few decades; for the rest of the time, people have communicated mostly with other people in small groups. We've said it before: Why we trust people is the same; it's only the ways we come to be trusted that have been changing, and that's because communication has been changing.

Of course, we could be wrong. But we're willing to bet that right now you and the people around you are concerned about the future. With newspapers, phone books, and video stores, along with a bunch of other dinosaur industries, going bankrupt, things are getting a bit worrisome. So why not try something new, like the stuff you have in your hands here? Often with experimentation, the downside is very small, while the possible reward is very large. So trying something new could do you worlds of good. You could hit upon small, new ways to connect or whole worlds of benefit and profit.

So give it a shot. Try something new today. It may just revolutionize what you do.

Trust us.

Index